HAUNTED HOUSES
OF
GREAT BRITAIN

The Haunted Manor of Abthorpe

HAUNTED HOUSES
OF
GREAT BRITAIN

JOSEPH BRADDOCK

Illustrated by
FELIX KELLY

DORSET PRESS
New York

All rights reserved.

This edition published by Dorset Press,
a division of Marboro Books Corporation,
by arrangement with
B. T. Batsford Ltd.
1991 Dorset Press

ISBN 0-88029-701-8

Printed in the United States of America

M 9 8 7 6 5 4 3 2 1

TO MY WIFE
who has walked with me round the
edge of the Unknown

PREFACE

A GREAT number of books has been written, in the present and in the past, about ghosts and haunted houses, linked with their allied subjects such as witchcraft, legends, miraculous cures, uncanny happenings at séances, extra-sensory perception, and visitations and messages received by living persons from the so-called dead. Therefore in a book belonging to this category, for which there would seem to be a perennial—perhaps significant—public demand, I cannot expect to be very original. But I have been selective in my fancy for the hauntings I shall relate, choosing the stories that follow not only for their strangeness, but also for their variety and contrast, and trying to arrange them in relation to each other so that the reader's attention and interest, I hope, need not flag; for writers must seek to entertain: "Unless they please they are not heard at all." And I hope, further, that my own viewpoint, my particular angle on the supernormal world may add some colour and personal flavour to my material.

George Orwell is reported to have once said: "The problem of the world is this: Can we get men to behave decently to each other if they no longer believe in God?" But it is possible that those outside the revealed religions tend to exaggerate reports of the death of belief in God. Orwell also wrote:

> No bomb that ever burst
> Shatters the crystal spirit.

He could have said "Christian spirit"; yet, writing quite undenominationally as an anti-materialist, I will simply state my own belief in a world of spirit which is just as real as this one, with my conviction that our behaviour to each other here and now directly affects the degree of happiness or pain we shall find in a future life. In other words I must believe in the psychic operation of cause and effect, in Karma, and in the existence of Good and Evil. I believe in a purposeful force behind the universe.

Such belief, of course, makes it easier to credit the reality of

PREFACE

certain ghosts or spirits. But, as we shall see, there are different kinds of ghosts. I should like to ask the reader to try and keep an open mind as to the truth, or otherwise, of each tale of haunting; while, if possible, accepting the principle of the supremacy of the World of the Spirit over the world of matter, as the single antidote to the menace of a short-sighted materialism which is threatening to destroy the earth.

ACKNOWLEDGMENT

I should like to express my sincere thanks to the following for their kind and generous help in providing me with material for this book, or lending me books for reference:

Mrs. Bailey, Mickledown, Reigate Road, Ewell, Surrey; Major and Mrs. George Anne, Draycott House, Roedean Way, Brighton; Major Ian Murray, Foxes Bank, Wadhurst, Sussex; Mr. R. H. D'Elboux, Whitelands, Battle, Sussex; Miss Sylvia Calmady-Hamlyn, Perroc Vean, Buckfastleigh, South Devon; Mrs. Olive Hodgkinson, Wookey Hole, Wells, Somerset; Mrs. Robin Clerk, Rose Cottage, Knapp, Somerset; Mrs. Verner-Jeffreys, Ewhurst, Surrey; Mr. Walter Taylor, Editor, *The Western Independent*, Plymouth; Miss Ruth Thomas, Yannon Tower, Teignmouth, Devonshire; Mr. W. H. Paynter, 18, Castle Street, Liskeard, Cornwall; Miss Daphne du Maurier, Menabilly, Par, Cornwall; Mrs. Morier, New House, Penshurst, Kent; Mr. Hugh Dent, 1, Shaftesbury Villas, Ford Park, Plymouth; Dr. Sybil Hawkes, Rostrevor, Mannamead, Plymouth; Mr. and Mrs. Harrold Collier, 46a, Holland Park, London; Mr. "Laddie" Richardson and Mr. Frank Killick, Burwash, Sussex; Mr. Roger Frewen, Brede Place, Near Rye, Sussex; Mr. Percy White, 17, Watchbell Street, Rye, Sussex; Mr. S. J. Holloway, Reysons Farm, Broad Oak, Rye, Sussex; Mr. George Bullock, St. Lucy's, Church Square, Rye, Sussex; Major Patrick Grant, Woodlands, Heathfield, Sussex; Mr. R. Thurston Hopkins, 11, Richmond Street, Brighton; Mr. Rupert Gunnis, Hungershall House, Hungershall Park, Tunbridge Wells; Miss Noel Streatfeild, 51a, Elizabeth Street, Eaton Square, London; Miss Irene Carr, The Old Vicarage, Westham, Pevensey, Sussex; Mr. W. Macqueen-Pope,

PREFACE

Coventry House, 5-6, Coventry Street, London; Mr. Raymond Mander and Mr. Joe Mitchenson, 5, Venner Road, Sydenham, London; Mrs. Ruth Freeman, Barn Cottage, Pembury, Kent; Mr. and Mrs. Leslie Phillips, The Holman Clavel Inn, Culmhead, Taunton, Somerset; Mr. G. W. Copeland, 23, Carfrae Terrace, Mount Gould, Plymouth; Mr. and Mrs. Maurice Tate, the Greyhound Hotel, Wadhurst, Sussex; Mr. and Mrs. Hilary Ball, The King's Arms Hotel, Rotherfield, Sussex; Mr. Roy Grigg, The Grenadier, 18, Wilton Row, London; Mr. Fred Archer, Editor, *Pyschic News*, 144, High Holborn, London; The Rev. W. H. Stevens, Glen Millans, Ambleside, Westmorland; Mr. Stuart Legg, Braemar, The Holt, Farnham, Surrey; Mrs. Priestley, Newhouse Farm, Tidebrook, Wadhurst, Sussex; Mr. H. R. Hardy, Edgeborough, Frensham, Surrey; and the Rev. R. Bathurst Ravenscroft and Mr. L. E. Stotesbury-Leeson, Calverton Rectory, Wolverton, Buckinghamshire.

The Extract on page 46 is quoted, by permission, from CASTLES by Sir Charles Oman, K.B.E., published by the Great Western Railway in 1926.

My thanks are also due to *George Allen and Unwin Ltd.* for permission to quote from THE STORY OF MY LIFE by Augustus Hare; to *Mr. Hereward Carrington* for permission to quote from his paper, Fifth International Psychical Congress, Oslo, 1935; to *Burns Oates & Washbourne Ltd.* for permission to quote from GHOSTS AND POLTERGEISTS by Father Herbert Thurston, S.J.; to *Professor Hornell Hart, Ph.D., M.A.* for permission to quote from his series of articles APPARITIONS AND GHOSTLY VISITATIONS; to *Psychic Press Ltd.* for permission to quote from THE CHELTENHAM GHOST by B. Abdy Collins; to *Methuen & Co. Ltd.* for permission to quote from THE HAUNTING OF CASHEN'S GAP by Harry Price and R. S. Lambert; to *Rider & Co.* for permission to quote from THE TRUTH ABOUT THE TALKING MONGOOSE by Nandor Fodor in THE STORY OF THE POLTERGEIST DOWN THE AGES by Harry Price and R. S. Lambert; to *Mrs. Edith R. Jones* for permission to quote from STEPHEN CRANE AT BREDE published in the Atlantic Monthly in 1954.

CONTENTS

	PAGE
Preface	7
List of Illustrations	11

CHAPTER
- I THE FRINGE OF THE UNKNOWN . . 13
- II GHOSTS AT BURGHWALLIS HALL, YORKSHIRE 27
- III SOME HAUNTED CASTLES. . . . 41
- IV A WEST COUNTRY GHOST-HUNT . . 59
- V MISCELLANEOUS POLTERGEISTS . . 81
- VI BREDE PLACE, RYE, AND REYSONS FARM. 101
- VII THE CHELTENHAM GHOST: MRS. GASKELL'S GHOST STORY, AND A SPANISH CODA . 117
- VIII EVIL HAUNTINGS 135
- IX THE REMARKABLE MONGOOSE. . . 155
- X THEATRE GHOSTS 171
- XI HAUNTED PUBS, AND THE RUNCORN POLTERGEIST 187
- XII PHOTOGRAPHS OF GHOSTS AND CONCLUSION 203

LIST OF ILLUSTRATIONS

The Haunted Manor of Abthorpe   *Frontispiece*

Haslingden. "... a pink-globed popping gas-jet on the landing, the glazed brown wallpaper in the rather dingy bathroom." *page* 21

Burghwallis Hall. "... a small woman in a dark dress walking along the corridor between the Billiards Room and the Chapel."   33

Herstmonceux Castle, Sussex.   53

Buckfast Abbey. "Looking round, he saw a number of monks walking in Indian file and in perfect silence."   65

"He lived at a house in Bryn-terrace, Llanelly, until driven away by an apparition which appeared at their bedside at midnight on Thursday, June 2nd."   93

Brede Place, Sussex.   109

"The figure was that af a tall lady, dressed in black of a soft woollen material, judging from the slight sound in moving."   123

"A few miles away from our cantonments was a steep hill crowned with a half-ruined fort many hundred years old..."   137

"Doarlish Cashen... is an ancient, bleak and remote farmhouse..."   157

Drury Lane: the Man in Grey   173

"The boy complained of the shadow of a person reflected upon his bedroom wall... advancing and retreating like someone hesitating to come in."   193

"... the photograph clearly showed, looking over a tuft of grass on the far side of the road, a little girl of about five or six years old."   211

HAUNTED HOUSES
OF
GREAT BRITAIN

"The Brothers spoke of Ghosts,—a favourite theme
With those who love to reason or to dream;
And they, as greater men were wont to do,
Felt strong desire to think the stories true."
George Crabbe: Lady Barbara; or The Ghost

"Millions of spiritual Creatures walk the Earth
Unseen, both when we wake, and when we sleep."
John Milton: Paradise Lost: Book IV

Chapter One

The Fringe of the Unknown

AT the outset I will admit, a little sadly, that I have never seen a ghost. I may have heard one. It would be nice to have some visual confirmation of one's beliefs; but, after all, we have to accept a great deal in this life on the evidence of others. A majority of the findings of modern science has to be accepted on trust by the layman. And many things that we know exist—light, electricity, poetry, for examples—almost defy definition. Boswell records that Dr. Johnson was once asked "What is poetry?" "Why, Sir," Johnson replied with characteristic common sense, "it is much easier to say what it is not. We all *know* what light is; but it is not easy to *tell* what it is." And so with electricity and poetry, it is difficult to know simply and exactly what they are; but we know what they do, we recognise the symptoms of the power that is in them. When A. E. Housman, author of *A Shropshire Lad*, was asked in America to define poetry, he gave this answer: "I replied that I could no more define poetry than a terrier can define a rat, but that I thought we both recognised the object by the symptoms which it provokes in us. One of these symptoms was described in connexion with another object by Eliphaz the Temanite: 'A spirit passed before my face: the hair of my flesh stood up.'" It is strange to find Housman equating his reaction to poetry with the sensations of one of Job's comforters in face of a ghostly visitation, but the point is that ghosts, if they exist, are spirits who elude definition and hate being pinned down. But they produce symptoms still, today as in the past:

> Fear came upon me, and trembling,
> Which made all my bones to shake.
> Then a spirit passed before my face;
> The hair of my flesh stood up.
> It stood still, but I could not discern the appearance thereof;
> A form was before mine eyes.

When I say that I have never seen a ghost, this is true. Yet I was, as it were, brought up within the ambience of one. Every Christmas—surely the right season for ghosts—until I was about twelve years old, I spent a few weeks with my parents and my brother and the family of my maternal grand-parents in the East Lancashire manufacturing town of Haslingden, a place of tall chimneys and cobbled streets, where the house, Tor View, overlooked on one side some bleak enough moorland country. Tor View, I know now, used to be haunted. I will give the brief facts about this Lancashire ghost presently.

Belief in ghosts of one sort or another (for we must take into account such different alleged manifestations as subjective and hallucinatory phantoms, phantasms of the living, materialisations of deceased persons, earthbound souls, automatic types of apparition, poltergeists and elementals) has been found in every age and country. One should add that scepticism also about the genuineness of ghostly appearances is as old and universal as belief. But a thing that has puzzled me in the world today has been the still generally hostile attitude to psychic phenomena of most orthodox scientists and many orthodox leaders of religion. In his Foreword to Sir Ernest Bennett's *Apparitions and Haunted Houses: A Survey of Evidence*, The Very Rev. W. R. Matthews, The Dean of St. Paul's, writes: "The attitude of the 'orthodox' man of science to 'psychic phenomena' is extraordinary. For the most part he ignores the existence of the evidence; when compelled to recognise it he writes it down as a tissue of error and deceit. Yet there are facts which appear to be well attested and which, if true, would throw a new light upon the nature of existence. Telepathy alone, without the hypothesis of telepathic communication with the dead, must have quite revolutionary consequences when its implications are thought out." And from the Christian point of view the Dean of St. Paul's comments that "it would be a great gain for spiritual religion if some fresh evidence could be discovered that consciousness is not wholly dependent on the body and extinguished when the body dies."

Anyone who is willing to study the *Proceedings* of the Society for Psychical Research with an open mind, will, I think, find out that there is plenty of first-hand evidence, cumulative and corroborative, evidence that is of compelling weight for belief in the supernormal. The S.P.R., as I shall from now on call it, was founded in London in 1882 by the efforts of Professor Barrett and a group of distinguished Cambridge men, including Frederic Myers, the eminent philosopher Professor Henry Sidgwick and, perhaps not so generally known, Alfred Tennyson, to make "an organised and scientific attempt to investigate that large group of debatable phenomena designated by such terms as psychical and spiritualistic." And three years later an American S.P.R. was founded in New York under the leadership of the psychologist William James. It is interesting that in 1889 Tennyson published "The Ring," a poem on an unusually psychic theme, which contained a definite statement of belief:

> The ghost in man, the ghost that once was man
> But cannot wholly free itself from Man,
> Are calling to each other thro' a dawn
> Stranger than earth has ever seen; the veil
> Is rending, and the Voices of the day
> Are heard across the Voices of the dark.

However, at the close of the nineteenth century, in spite of the interest in psychical investigation stimulated by the rapid advance and materialistic claims of physics, the scientific world as a whole remained hostile. Scientists denied the facts, declined to investigate, and "called believers superstitious fools." As Dr. D. J. West, a qualified medical man who has been for many years an Experimental Research Officer to the S.P.R., goes on to say in his recent book *Psychical Research Today*: "Thomas Huxley, answering an invitation from a committee of the London Dialectical Society to join with them in an investigation of spiritualistic phenomena, replied that he was no more interested in their offer than he would be interested in an offer to listen in to the chatter of old women and curates in a distant cathedral town."

But today, in the middle of the twentieth century, those of us who have lived through the marvels and agonies of the last fifty years or so feel less sure of ourselves, less arrogant. Confronted by violence and terrible wars, by the shocking breakdown of moral sense in a return to torture and mass extermination, we are threatened with nuclear annihilation; yet we see all round us the daily evidence of miracles and mysteries such as radar, television, the preparations for interplanetary exploration, and wonder whether man may not be on the threshold of vast new knowledge. We are aware that the human race is not old. The little creature, Man, has lived through only a minuscule of Time. And civilisation on our tiny planet, Earth, extends no farther back than a few thousand years; and modern science, as we know it, only a few hundreds.

In the ante-chapel of Trinity College, Cambridge, the statue of Sir Isaac Newton bears perhaps Newton's finest memorial, those lines from Wordsworth's "The Prelude":

> The marble index of a mind for ever
> Voyaging through strange seas of Thought alone.

Newton once compared himself to a child picking up pebbles on the shores of an infinite ocean. Tennyson, faced with the insoluble mystery of the universe, compared himself to

> An infant crying in the night;
> An infant crying for the light;
> And with no language but a cry.

Fortunately, in the free world at least, there are welcome signs of a shift away from the cramped and closed philosophy of materialism; a sense of new beginnings in new sciences that belong to the mind and soul of man. After the probings of psychology, the findings of Freud and Jung, there is more willingness on the part of many, including eminent scholars and scientists, to allow that there could be, perhaps, more things in heaven and earth than were dreamt of in the science of Huxley, Darwin, or Sir James Frazer; even, possibly, to admit an honest ghost or two. *The Golden Bough* has lost its lustre. It is conceivable that, before this century is out, some of the most sensational fresh discoveries may well be made in the realms of an already established psychic science.

The first professorial chair in psychical research was recently founded, rather surprisingly not in England or America where most of the pioneer work was done, but in Holland at the University of Utrecht. Dr. West writes: "Far-seeing thinkers, from Socrates to Henry Sidgwick and Albert Einstein, have not doubted the importance of the investigation of psychic phenomena, and the Presidential Chair of the 'Society for Psychical Research' has been graced by a galaxy of distinguished persons. Psychical researchers stand on the edge of a new, exciting world that invites bold exploration. Only recently have the methods of scientific experimentation been applied to the task. Already the yield is remarkable, but it is only the beginning ... we are only on the fringe of great things."

Although psychical research today is full of such tremendous possibilities, the whole subject is still an inquiry into the unknown, a big unanswered question mark. In spite of the distinguished work done in all civilised countries—by Flammarion in France, by Professor Bozzano in Italy, by Dr. Walter Prince in the U.S.A., but most of all in Britain—the chief barrier now is far less a matter of prejudice than a lack of funds. Psychical research needs to be admitted as an important subject for study in the universities everywhere, so that students can be properly trained for a lifetime's work in this field. Who could say then what assurances, what great benefits might not be revealed to humanity?

For the bearing it may have on ghosts and hauntings by the spirits of the departed, we may remember what that well-known physicist and spiritualist, Sir Oliver Lodge, has said and written: "I tell you with all the strength of conviction that I can muster that we do persist, that people still continue to take an interest in what is going on, that they know far more about things on this earth than we do, and are able from time to time to communicate with us." And in his book *The Destiny of Man* he sums up a portion of his other-worldly philosophy as follows: "Man now knows that though related to the animals on his bodily side, he is related to quite other Beings on his mental and spiritual side. He has developed a religious sense which teaches him that he is actually in touch with a higher order of Creation, that he can have intercourse with it, that he can derive thence help and comfort; that he is not isolated or stranded, nor temporary and evanescent, but that he has within him the seed of Immortality; that on the spiritual side his roots go down to infinite depths, and that he may blossom into regions supernal. It is not truly scientific to ignore this instinct, or any other psychological fact."

In such good company as I have mentioned, then, and in the face of powerful unknown forces much greater than ourselves, we can surely afford to take our ghost stories seriously, careless of ridicule, without fear of loss of face. If, as we shall find, there would seem to be evil ghosts and evil vibrations, this is because men with free will, in working out their destinies, sometimes do evil as well as good. While we consider the accounts of the supernormal happenings that follow, let us resolve to steer a middle course, which is to adopt a mental attitude neither gullibly credulous nor bone-headedly sceptical. If any superior person should ask us outright, with scornful disapproval: "But do you believe in magic?" we might do worse than return them the answer of a simple man, that humble confectioner, Hassan of Baghdad, who (as all of us must eventually) came to make the Golden Journey to Samarkand: "Men who think themselves wise believe nothing till the proof. Men who are wise believe anything till the disproof." And negative proof is a difficult matter.

Now to return to the ghost at Haslingden. There is not much

to tell, but that there was a ghost I am certain. Tor View, which stood on the crest of a steep narrow lane, was one of two attached grey stone houses that had originally been three Victorian cottages. Looking back to childhood Christmases spent there, the house does seem suitable for a ghost! In retrospect there is a period flavour. I remember so well how we used to arrive at Haslingden station: the "fly" waiting for us, with its musty, almost indescribable smell; sitting on a worn leather seat next to my brother, peering through the ill-fitting, snow-plastered window and seeing snow on the mill-girls' shawls pinched tightly round their heads, hearing the clop-clop of the horse on the snow-flurried Lancashire cobbles. The cab turned into the lane, the horse would soon begin to walk, and then presently I could make out a vague amber patch of light—Tor View above us in front, as the cab creaked and wobbled. The house inside was friendly, old-fashioned, and details about it remain clearly in my memory: downstairs, a long narrow passage and the warm stone-floored kitchen; a pink-globed popping gas-jet on the landing, the glazed brown wallpaper in the rather dingy bathroom; and the nine sharp steps leading up to the attic, with a large toy-cupboard going right under the roof, where my brother and I slept. We tried hard to see the ghost, but we never did. Such was the setting. Here are the facts as far as I know them.

The original cottages most probably were built in the 'thirties or 'forties of last century. A family named Walton first lived in the house that was Tor View, and there was a daughter Emma who is rumoured to have died young after some luckless love affair. My maternal grandparents moved into the house from Oldham in 1893 when my mother was nineteen years old, for the reason that her father, John Hyde Bailey, had been appointed manager of the Haslingden branch of the District Banking Company. I remember my grandfather—he died when I was twelve—as a dreamer, a dapper man, with a trim white beard, a bright complexion and studious eyes. I know him now to have been a gentle soul, with a great taste for poetry, who knew the sonnets of Shakespeare by heart. His early years had been spent just over the border in the borough of Glossop in Derbyshire.

My mother, the only daughter, had five brothers all younger than herself, whom she had largely helped Mrs. Bailey to bring up. From 1893 until 1897, when at the age of twenty-three she married and went south to live near London, she must have been the central focus of that household. The ghost was seen on many occasions by various members of the family, at all hours of the day or night, from shortly after my mother left home until as late as 1921, when the house was given up. As the ghost took the form of a young woman of about my mother's modest height and build and never in the least alarmed anybody, rather giving an impression of a singular, subdued sweetness, I had wondered at first whether this wasn't, perhaps, a phantasm of the living, a visual projection of my mother's personality induced telepathically by her. But it would only have been during the early years of her marriage that her image might have nostalgically haunted her home.

Here, in passing, I should perhaps mention that the Rev. Dodd, the then Vicar of St. Peter's Church, Laneside, and Mr. Bailey lived in adjoining houses and that the Bailey boys, with more high spirits than unkindness, sometimes tried to frighten Lucy Dodd, the vicar's daughter, by telling her that the ghost had been seen to pass through the wall into her house. But it was never seen, so far as I know, by any member of the Dodd family.

The Haslingden ghost was seen by Mr. and Mrs. Bailey, by Harry Bailey, the eldest son who became Rector of Denton and later Vicar of Walkden, by Miss Elsie Yerkess who at the time was engaged to marry Will Bailey, the youngest of the brothers, and by Laura, the servant at Tor View. Harry Bailey, who was educated at Jesus College, Cambridge, was cultured, level-headed and extremely matter-of-fact. The only time I asked him about the ghost, he asserted its reality in two laconic words: "It exists." This went far to convince me. He had seen the shape of the lady come out of the maid's little room on the first floor and go into the bathroom.

One Christmas season (somewhere about 1912 it must have been) Mr. Bailey had a favourite cousin of his, Jinnie, staying in the house. Mrs. Bailey had gone into the kitchen before supper

Haslingden. "... a pink-globed popping gas-jet on the landing, the glazed brown wallpaper in the rather dingy bathroom."

to take some mince-pies out of the oven, and as she was on her way back to the dining-room she saw cousin Jinnie go upstairs. She opened the door, and there was cousin Jinnie sitting comfortably in an arm-chair talking to Mr. Bailey. "Why, Jinnie, but I've just seen you going upstairs!" she said. "You never have," cousin Jinnie retorted, "for I haven't left this chair." "But," said Mrs. Bailey, "I heard the stairs creak!"

Now that was a funny thing. My Aunt Elsie—formerly Miss Yerkess—speaking of the ghost and of another apparition, that of John Hyde Bailey, which she claims to have seen, said to me: "When either ghost went up or downstairs, the sound was quite clear—those stairs *creaked*. And there used to be wicker chairs in the house, too, and sometimes they would creak, as though somebody had just got up out of them."

My Aunt Elsie, the only direct witness of the female phantom who is still alive, has given me a pretty coherent account of what she saw. She can offer no explanation for this gentle haunting, but herself believes that the ghost may have been the spirit of Emma Walton still bound to the scene of some thwarted or tragic love affair. The period would seem to be right. This is what she told me:

"I saw her many times, twice for instance in 1918, for she was moving backwards and forwards about the house frequently. I should say she was about five foot three or four inches in height; and she looked dainty, yet something like an old photograph that is fading. But you couldn't see through her, no she looked quite solid and she was always dressed in an early Victorian style. She had fair hair parted down the middle and drawn back in a bun on her neck. Once I saw her go to a big wardrobe in the bedroom and then move away; after a short interval, the door of the wardrobe swung open as though she hadn't shut it properly. One summer morning I woke up and it was already light and I saw her, where she stood at the end of my bed. She smiled at me in a sad way. She was wearing a long grey flimsy dress, with buttons down the front. I saw the hem of her full skirt stir as she made a movement with her foot. She looked so pretty and sweet, I had no fear. I didn't feel cold or anything. Oh, she *was* sweet! Her hands were folded over each other, until she put her hands on the bed and smiled sadly. She had lovely hands. Then she moved over to the wall next to the Dodd's house and she went suddenly out, just like a candle."

My grandfather died in July, 1914, eighteen months after his retirement, following fifty years' service with the Banking Company. He had looked forward to some travelling in Europe, but he was not to realise this ambition. However, he had the comforts both of religion and philosophy, so he had accepted his fate with a stoical calm. As I have written elsewhere: "Later, I learnt that my grandfather, finding his illness mortal, had refused to undergo a major operation which would have prolonged his life.... I gathered that the last weeks of his life had not been unhappy ... he had his poets. He might almost be said to have left this world to the diapason of Shakespeare's sonnets."

Laura vowed that she saw "the Master" on several occasions after his death. Once when Elsie Yerkess, as she still was, stood in the kitchen at Tor View with her back to the door, while Laura finished making the toast, the maid seemed suddenly to stiffen. She was sitting before the toasting fire, her knees apart, her good-natured, normally rosy polished face scarlet from the heat, a wisp of hair falling across her nose; so my aunt has painted the picture. "Ah, there's Master, just gone up the stairs," Laura remarked, without too much emphasis. "And what's more he's rubbing his hands together as he always used to do."

Elsie Yerkess in August 1914 was troubled and unhappy, because my grandmother was bitterly opposed to her engagement to Will Bailey. She was even wondering whether it wouldn't be for the best to give up her engagement. She lived at Colne, and one night during this August she had gone to bed unusually early, about 8 p.m., and was lying on her side in bed worrying over her problem, trying to decide what to do about Mrs. Bailey's hostility. After, possibly, half an hour, she saw the bedroom door slide open and a figure that she instantly recognised, beyond doubt, move up to her bedside. The figure was all in white, dressed in a shroud with long sleeves, tied round with a beautiful shiny silken girdle that had thick silk tassels, one of which trailed on the floor. She cried out: "Oh, Mr. Bailey!" and then he gave her a very sweet smile.

All the same, she has told me, she was terrified, feeling the conventional sensations one is expected to feel in such circumstances, an icy shiver lifting each hair of her head, a horrid thrill through all her body. The apparition was at the side of the bed and all at once unexpectedly stretched out a hand and stroked her in one majestic sweep from her face down to her foot. The touch on her face was cold, and she was still more frightened. The phantom passed to the end of the bed. Now, hanging its arms down loosely along its sides, it rose up slowly to the ceiling where it faded right out.

But the next day Elsie Yerkess was able to feel the visitation as a comfort, an intended reassurance. After consulting with her mother, she decided not to break off her engagement.

Chapter Two

Ghosts at Burghwallis Hall, Yorkshire

SOME extraordinary, most varied, and quite recent facts of hauntings at Burghwallis Hall, near Doncaster, were given to me by my friend Major George Anne, who, until lately, was owner-heir of this historic Catholic Hall and Shrine, and by his wife Constance Anne, when they were living at Bardown, a house near to me at Ticehurst. The Annes are a very old Roman Catholic family, who originally came from Normandy to Yorkshire, and whose descent can be traced back to three generations before 1266. But before I come to give a precise account of the strange matters which were revealed to me by Major and Mrs. Anne, perhaps some of the atmosphere and historical detail surrounding Burghwallis Hall will not be out of place.

The house will always remain a shrine of the ancient faith because of its connexion with the Venerable John Anne, who suffered martyrdom at York in 1588. In *Forgotten Shrines*, An Account of Some Old Catholic Halls and Families in England and of Relics and Memorials of the English Martyrs, by Dom Bede Cam, it is related that "Dr. Champneys, who was a witness of the martyrdom, was very greatly impressed by the meekness and constancy shown by the blessed man and his fellow martyr, Venerable Robert Dalby. At their trial 'one Bramley, a felon, saw hanging over their heads a great round light which every time they spake would, as it were, move itself, and at the end of their speeches vanish away.' This converted the man, and he died with the martyrs, a good Catholic and sincere penitent."

However, it was not the Venerable John Anne himself who had lived at Burghwallis Hall but his sister. John Anne was born at Frickley, some five miles from Burghwallis, a moated dwelling destroyed by fire about two hundred years ago, which was then the home of the Annes. The ancient family chapel once attached to the Hall at Frickley has also nearly disappeared, only very insignificant ruins today marking the place where, for some hundreds of years, Mass had been celebrated. It was only after a Michael Anne sold Frickley during the eighteenth century that Burghwallis Hall finally became the family residence.

Major George Anne's mother, who was the lady of the house at the beginning of this present century, has given an account of Burghwallis Hall, from which the selections that follow may help the reader to build up the right picture:

"Burghwallis Hall (anciently Burgh Wallis) was built in the fourteenth century, and has been added to from time to time. It has been the property of the Annes for more than 400 years, and has had a Catholic mission attached to it ever since the venerable parish church was taken out of the rightful owners' possession, in the sixteenth century. The Hall was formerly a picturesque gabled manor house with the large Hall and heavily timbered roof found in those early days, and the fine old ceiling with its oak beams is still to be seen running through the main part of the older portion of the building. . . .

"It is believed that there was a chapel in some sequestered spot at Burghwallis, erected almost immediately after the ejection of the Catholics from their churches, for an old door, now belonging to one of the cottages on the estate, is still spoken of as 'the door of the old chapel.' No vestige of any building, however, remains. In the hidden chapel, wherever it may have been, the Venerable martyr will often have celebrated Mass, and we may suppose that he wore those very vestments which now lie tattered and stained with age in the drawers of the Sacristy, and used the old Missal printed at Antwerp in 1576....

"In the house are many treasures relating to the past. One is a portrait of George Leyburne, President of Douay College from 1652 to 1670; the other is a beautiful oil-painting of Bishop John Leyburne, the first Vicar-Apostolic, who on being sent by the Pope to England, lost no time but went at a gallop through the northern counties, and confirmed 20,000 people in two months.... In the library the furniture dates back hundreds of years, and some fine specimens of oak carving belonging to the fifteenth and sixteenth centuries are to be found among the high-backed chairs. There is also a quaint old fifteenth-century table. The book-shelves contain a great number of old missals, breviaries, and books of piety, in whose fly-leaves may be read such names as Gage, Fitzherbert, Killingbeck, Clifford, Cholmeley, Needham, Vavasour, Brackenbury, Philip Hamerton, Father James Meynell, and many of the Annes.

"In 1907, in taking some measurements in the attics, a small chamber was discovered to which there was no access except by crawling along a very narrow space under the roof for a distance of some twenty yards. This chamber measures seven or eight feet square, and was empty, but it was so constructed that anyone in the room would think that the space was the well of the staircase adjoining. A builder who has seen it can give no explanation why it was made, as it is not in any way necessary to the construction of the building.

"Burghwallis is the mother mission of the whole neighbourhood: in fact Burghwallis has always been Catholic. The date of the present chapel, an unpretentious addition to the house in red brick, is uncertain, but its very unecclesiastical appearance outside, and its unobtrusive public entrance—up a narrow flight of stone steps in the back yard—point to its having been built in penal times, probably some time early in the eighteenth century."

Cardinal Newman, in one of his great sermons, has treated with fine eloquence the theme of the decay of the Catholic Church in this country, and of its miraculous resurrection. "No longer the Catholic Church in the country; nay, no longer, I may say a Catholic community; but a few adherents of the Old Religion, moving silently and sorrowfully about, as memorials of what had been.... There, perhaps, an elderly person, seen walking in the streets, grave and solitary, and strange, though noble in bearing, and said to be of good family and a 'Roman Catholic.' An old-fashioned house of gloomy appearance, closed in with high walls, with an iron gate and yews, and the report attaching to it that 'Roman Catholics' lived there; but who they were, or what was meant by calling them Roman Catholics, no one could tell; though it had an unpleasant sound and told of form and superstition." Englishmen of all creeds are far more tolerant and sympathetic today, knowing more of the barren winter of the spirit which any senseless persecution brings. But these ancient halls and manor houses, once the homes and refuges of temporarily lost causes, do still possess an undefinable air of mystery and romance that seems to breathe from their old weather-worn walls which are "half as old as Time!" They must always, I think, move sensitive people to feelings of wonder and curiosity. Of such is Burghwallis Hall, until recently the home of the Annes.

Major Anne is in his late sixties, straightforward, with a slightly bluff kindness and warm geniality. While both he and his wife, a good deal younger than he is and possessing a great charm of manner, are Roman Catholics, they are not obtrusively religious, but strike one as sensible people prepared to enjoy the best things of life, both with a quick sense of humour. Major Anne is interested in horse-racing and wears sporting country clothes. They are not, in fact, the sort of people that one would at first associate with an interest in occult phenomena; or with seeing ghosts. The account which follows of what happened at Burghwallis Hall during the last war, is based upon notes pencilled by Major Anne in 1944 and most kindly given to me with permission to use them as I liked.

The story harks back. Before 1939 Major Anne had, at one time or another, occupied every bedroom at Burghwallis, except the Landing Room which was always used by his father. But he had never, at any time during the course of his fifty or more years, either heard or seen the slightest sign of a ghost. As was inevitable with such an old house, the subject of possible ghosts had periodically come up for discussion. Major Anne's father always said that Burghwallis was entirely free of ghosts; and he, at least, must have had an open mind on the subject, because he was one of the few people who saw the celebrated White Lady of Blenkinsopp Castle in Northumberland.

Major Anne's mother always laughed at any suggestion that Burghwallis might be haunted. She invariably spoke of the old place as having the most "peaceful atmosphere" she knew. She died in 1937, aged eighty. However, it should be recorded that she once told Major Anne that she had seen "a small woman in a dark dress" walking along the corridor between the Billiards Room and the Chapel. Upon another occasion she described to him how, lying in bed in the Garden Room with the door open, she had heard sounds of music, "like a musical-box," coming from the Billiards Room opposite. This occurred long before the days of radio, his recollection being that the same thing happened on several occasions and that his mother enjoyed it. She told one or two other people about it.

In 1904 Burghwallis Hall was let to the late Charles Brook, whose business had to do with the making of Brooks's cotton-reels, and who was at that time Master of the Badsworth Hounds. Major Anne, then a youth of eighteen, went to stay with him for four days and remembers him perfectly as a typical huntsman with a charming matter-of-fact personality. Charles Brook owned—that then *rara avis*—a motor-car, and took George Anne for his very first ride in a car to see his hounds in the Kennels at Badsworth five miles away, a fairly hazardous journey for a car in the first years of the century! But what Major Anne also remembers is that Brook complained to him quite bitterly about Burghwallis being "haunted," as if he, being the eldest son of his Landlord, could be held in some way responsible! Apparently, it was the *noises* that upset Charles Brook, strange, odd noises that kept upsetting his peace at night.

"During my visit to Brook at Burghwallis in 1904," writes Major Anne, "I had the Oak Room, which is in the oldest part of the house. Just as I was going off to sleep one night, there was a single resounding knock on my door. Whether this was a demonstration by some poltergeist, or was merely Brook getting a bit of his own back I can't say. I can only remember being thoroughly frightened. I have since used the Oak Room at various times, often for months on end, yet have never since experienced anything uncanny while in it."

Major Anne's eldest son Michael and his daughter Barbara shared a very odd experience in 1926, when they were about fifteen and fourteen years old. Brother and sister had been to the Chapel to say their prayers before dinner, and had cut the time rather fine. As they walked back along the long corridor they were afraid that they might be a little late and spoke of this to each other. At that moment they *both* saw the figure of a man come on to the landing from the Main Staircase; cross the landing away from them and go quickly up into the South Wing by a small staircase, at the top of which the figure turned sharply to the right. Neither of them caught sight of the face; but the figure was wearing a grey out-door suit of clothes and Barbara said to Michael: "That's Daddy—so we're not late." Arrived in the front Hall, they saw that dinner was on the point of being served so they went straight into the dining-room, where they found everybody who was staying at Burghwallis already assembled, including their father, and all the men were in *evening dress!* There were no menservants at Burghwallis at that time. Both the children experienced a very pronounced shock. Neither of them mentioned the occurrence to Major Anne at the time; but neither of them has ever forgotten it. It might be a significant coincidence that this happened on December 2nd, the anniversary of the death of Major Anne's brother, Bob, who was killed in action in 1917. But the most interesting and valuable part of this testimony is that it entirely refutes the argument so often brought forward for disbelieving in ghosts, that the

Burghwallis Hall. "... *a small woman in a dark dress walking along the corridor between the Billiards Room and the Chapel.*"

same ghost is never seen by two or more people at the same time.

Major Anne's father died on November 25th, 1939, in the Landing Room. The next part of Major Anne's story centres round the Landing Room, which he occupied early in the year 1940. "If indeed what I saw and heard," he writes, "were the manifestations of some departed spirit, I feel quite certain that my old father had no part in them at all. He was far too good and kindly. Whereas most of the things which disturbed us were very much the reverse." I will let Major Anne tell his own experiences in his own words.

"On the 12th May, 1940, I was sitting in the Library at 11 p.m. The Library has a low ceiling and is below the Landing Room. I heard very loud footsteps stamping about overhead. I use the word 'stamping' because they sounded like the footsteps of a very angry person. I went quickly upstairs to find not a soul about. The servants had all retired to their quarters in a remote part of the house, and Constance was abed in the Ivy Room (which adjoins the Landing Room, but is a bit higher up in the South Wing). I went on to her; she also had heard the disturbance and wondered what it was.

"On November 5th, 1940, I was reading in bed about 11 p.m. when I heard a really terrific noise downstairs in the front hall. Several doors opened and shut with a crash, including (so it seemed) the heavy front door, and I most distinctly heard muffled shuffling of feet and the sound of subdued talk. I at once went out on to the landing—the noises ceased the moment I opened my door and there was nobody about.

"The following night, November 6th, there occurred what I rate as a most peculiar phenomenon. I had just turned out my lamp preparatory to going to sleep, when I heard the Ivy Room door open. Then there was a shuffling sound, the murmur of a voice and the sound of a dog whimpering. After that came the noise of two cuts with a whip. I heard the Ivy Room door close, and all was thereafter quiet. Constance had her pug, Vicky, with her as usual in the Ivy Room; and at the time it only struck me as most strange that she should whip the paragon of perfection.

Next morning I taxed her at breakfast with cruelty to small dogs, and she was amazed. Of course she had never beaten Vicky, neither had she been out of bed. In fact she had been sound asleep during the happenings I have narrated. Nobody, except the maids, who slept in a remote part of the Hall, was then at Burghwallis."

During the three or four years that Major Anne and his wife were living at Burghwallis Hall, it is perhaps worth noting that two maidservants sleeping under the same roof were cousins, were both called Margaret, and were both about fourteen years old at the beginning of these weird events. We shall be looking at some interesting examples of what I will call "the poltergeist enigma" in later chapters; for, as Harry Price has stated, "nearly half of all reported cases of hauntings exhibit poltergeist characteristics." Many people are familiar today with the idea of the apparent connexion of poltergeist activity with adolescents, more generally with the puberty of girls, as though the poltergeist agent had succeeded in transmuting the tumultuous energies of the child's waking psyche at this period into kinetic energy. Here it is only necessary to say that noises of all kinds, sounds "like a musical box," knockings, stampings of angry footsteps, are typical poltergeist characteristics. But Major Anne shall come to the climax of his story.

"Although I have not got a note as to the exact date, about this time happened the most formidable experience of all. For the first, and I hope the last, time in my life I saw a Ghost, and, moreover, no prosaic spectre, but a thing fully in keeping with the most spooky of apparitions. It happened while I was sleeping in my quite modern, chromium-plated bed.

"I had been sound asleep, but I woke up pretty quickly feeling my bed being pushed very violently up and down on the right hand side. I saw a man almost bent over me, concentrated on bouncing my mattress up and down, and between each two or three pushes he lifted his head and looked at me. So long as I live I shall never, never forget the inexpressible expression of loathing, of intense hatred and malice on the countenance of this thing. The features were those of an old, very thin, clean-shaven man, with a rather long sharp nose. The thin lips were closely pressed together, conveying intense, mad, malignant hatred. I will never forget the wicked expression in the eyes, which I noticed most. I can see those evil eyes today exactly as I saw them that night years ago.

"I switched on my bedside lamp and all became normal. The fox-terrier, Sue, uncurled and stretched in the arm-chair; she apparently woke up as I put on the light. Poor feckless Sue then and there lost all reputation as a reliable ghost-guard!

"It was pitch dark when I saw this apparition, and anyone may well question how I could see it. The thing was, of course, self-luminous, not brightly so, but clear, with a greenish hue. I had an impression of some form of drapery. I have no explanation to offer, unless the ghost could possibly have been my great-grandfather, Michael Tasburgh, dressed in his shroud, who had somehow succeeded in probing into my deepest subconscious mind, or into the future, and knew of my intention to sell Burghwallis Hall a year before I did! Curiously enough, I was not unduly scared at the time. However, from that night onwards I never slept at Burghwallis without a lamp in my room."

During the year 1941 more mysterious noises were heard intermittently. On May 4th at 3 a.m. (1 a.m. G.M.T.) Major Anne was woken up by the loudest and most prolonged disturbance that he ever heard at Burghwallis. It came from the landing outside his bedroom and sounded, he has told me, exactly like someone driving large nails into a plank.

The pug—Vicky—was his guard that particular night and she barked loudly and set her hackles up. Constance Anne also heard this tremendous row from the Ivy Room. On August 1st, 1941, more than a year after the previous occasion, they had a repetition of the "angry footsteps." Soon after this Major Anne moved into the Oak Room, not because he was scared, but because the Landing Room had grown a bit draughty. He was never bothered by those strange noises again.

But on November 24th, 1941, when he was reading in the Library at about 10 p.m., he suddenly heard the front door of the hall shut with a terrific crash. His wife, who was in the kitchen regions, heard it clearly, too. Major Anne went straight to investigate and found the large, heavy front door standing wide open, and held back by the usual brass weight.

Mrs. Anne's experiences were different, and even more varied. From September, 1939, until they left Burghwallis three years later, she always occupied the Ivy Room in the South Wing. One night in October, 1939, she distinctly felt the presence of someone in the room, and on the following night this psychic impression grew even stronger until she began to think that she could make out the vague form of somebody; yet she wasn't absolutely certain. On the third night, however, an old lady appeared to Mrs. Anne, standing by the side of her bed and looking down at her with a very wistful expression on her face, and as though she wanted to say something. But the old lady never spoke.

Constance Anne talked to me about her experiences in her charming, positive, yet light-hearted way, with a characteristic absence of fuss which carried complete conviction. The old lady, she said, wore a grey coat, with a cape of the same material which reached to her waist. The coat was fastened with flat buttons covered with the same material. Her hat was something like a Salvation Army bonnet and she had very dark hair going grey, which showed in front of the bonnet. "I never saw her again," said Mrs. Anne, "but even after fourteen years I can clearly remember every detail of her appearance, that black and iron-grey hair, even her white eyelashes."

The next event did not occur until some months afterwards. Then one midnight Mrs. Anne woke up, hearing a noise, and suddenly the door of the Ivy Room opened and a young girl of about eleven came just into the bedroom. A boy, perhaps six or seven, smaller than the girl, was peeping round her shoulder. The girl had a fringe, cut in fair golden hair which fell to her shoulders and she kept hold of the handle of the door. She was half smiling. Both the children looked happy and completely natural. "They were flushed," says Mrs. Anne, "bright-eyed with natural excitement, just as if they had been playing some game and had come in to tell me all about it. After looking at me for a few moments, they went away and the door closed. I never saw the children again; but later on a visitor, who did not know what I had seen, described them as having appeared to him in the Porch Room."

During those war years when Mrs. Anne was at Burghwallis, she often saw a little white dog—somewhat like a Sealyham—with rather long curly hair and an undocked tail. This small dog always came into either the Drawing Room or the Library as she opened the doors of either of those rooms to go out. It would trot up and pass her, trot into the room and then disappear. She never heard it trotting and it never took any notice of her. Once she saw it in the Ivy Room. No dog of anything like its appearance belonged in the village. She saw it regularly for three years, frequently by daylight.

Once in the stillness of night in July, 1942, Constance Anne woke to see a man standing by the mantelpiece in the Ivy Room. He was wearing a brown coat with large, sagging pockets which had flaps, the sort of coat worn in Victorian days, and one pocket was bulging with papers. He was bent over as if searching for something, looking annoyed, and was passing his hand along the mantelshelf. He turned, stared hard at her in a bad-tempered way, and then all at once he vanished.

Mrs. Anne often heard rappings and other unaccountable sounds, as did her husband, on the landing and the loud, angry footsteps in the Landing Room. On August 5th, 1941, the Landing Room noises were extra loud and a guest, Miss Bridget Bailey, heard them, and that night the servants also complained of noises. This was the single time that the servants complained, except that an old Mrs. MacLoughlin, when she was taking care of the late Major Ernest Anne, mentioned various eerie disturbances. Miss Bridget Bailey asserted that once the door of her bedroom, the Porch Room, was violently burst open.

Yet, possibly, the most uncanny thing of all which happened to Mrs. Anne was when once, in the dead of night, she was kept awake for more than a couple of hours by steady, terrific noise on the stonework outside the Ivy Room. "It was," she explains, "the quite unmistakable sound of chisel upon stone, a loud, unpleasant, regular *tap*, *tap*, *tap*." So loud was it, in fact, that the next morning she asked the Rector, who lived only a few hundred yards away, whether he had heard anything. He had not, and neither had her husband. There was no accounting for this extraordinary phenomenon.

About a fortnight later the Annes paid a visit to a monumental mason's yard at Mexborough to order a headstone for Major Anne's parents' grave. A man was at work on a block of stone, and Mrs. Anne at once recognised an exact audible repetition of the sound she had heard in the night. What conceivably can have been the explanation? Could she have made some kind of psychic journey into the past, to the time when Burghwallis was being built—or into the almost immediate future at Mexborough? We cannot answer; but in this age of new science when we are told that concepts such as Space and Time may be illusory, except empirically upon one plane of our existence; in this century of man's psychical unfolding we may wonder....

But hauntings seldom last beyond what we must, perforce, call a period of time. Burghwallis Hall is still today in the hands of good Catholics, and I suspect that its ghosts are all laid. It is now named St. Anne's Convent and is run by a small devoted group of Roman Catholic nuns as a pleasant Home for Old Ladies.

Chapter Three

Some Haunted Castles

HAUNTED castles will always provide us with a diversion, a glance through magic casements into lands, if not of faery, then of history and legend most certainly forlorn; moreover legend which, though it will be likely to have acquired accretions, may well be rooted in fact. Whether the castle walls be prodigious Bamburgh in Northumberland, defying time and the elements and the North Sea; or those that have become a part of the crumbled ruins of Berry Pomeroy engulfed in trees down in lush Devonshire; or more happily glow in the mellowed pink brickwork of Herstmonceux rising peacefully from the waters of its placid moat in Sussex, all the castles of England, gaunt and forbidding, or lovely beyond description, offer much, as generation after generation has visited them, for the imagination to work on; yet it must be conceded that the sources of the tales of haunting date too far back for verification.

Hauntings would seem often to stem from basic weaknesses in human character, from what is dark or abject down to the commission of crime, murders, massacres, atrocities in one form or another. Two of the most powerful passions that have driven men to evil and despair are greed and lust; so in choosing to narrate a few "old, unhappy, far-off things" supposed to have happened in castles, which no doubt sometimes did happen, the story of "The White Lady of Blenkinsopp" comes first. Blenkinsopp Castle was built six centuries ago as a border stronghold upon a commanding knoll on the western frontier of Northumberland, and the legend that the phantom of "The White Lady"—a rival to "The White Lady of Skipsea Castle" in Yorkshire—haunts it, has persisted from very early times almost up to the present day.

Bryan de Blenkinsopp, as brave a man as could be wished, dependable for distinction in a border raid or upon the battlefield, had one fatal weakness, an inordinate greed for wealth. He cherished this obsession in secret, anxious never to give himself away; but his vice grew until it had become like a cancer in his soul.

At the marriage of a brother warrior, among the eager toasts that were drunk was one to Bryan de Blenkinsopp and his "ladye love." "Never," Sir Bryan inadvertently muttered, "never shall that be until I meet with a lady possessed of a chest of gold heavier than ten of my strongest men can carry into my castle." This unexpected announcement was received in shocked and disapproving silence. Angry and ashamed at having betrayed his unworthy secret, Sir Bryan forthwith quit the place and his country.

After many years he returned with a wife and a box of gold that took twelve strong men to carry into the castle. There was feasting, with rejoicing for the young lord's return, and the fame of his great wealth was great. But soon it became generally known that the life of the rich baron was by no means happy, for he and his wife continually quarrelled, because she, with the help of her foreign attendants, had hidden the chest of gold somewhere deep in the castle and refused to give it up to her lawful husband. Suddenly one day Sir Bryan left the castle and went no one knew whither.

For more than a year the lady was grief-stricken and filled the castle with her inconsolable shrieks. Servants were despatched to all parts of the world to try and find her husband, but without any success. Then Lady de Blenkinsopp set out herself, with her attendants, to look for the missing man. Neither of them was ever heard of again; so it is averred that the lady, tortured by remorse for her undutiful conduct, cannot rest in her grave. She is doomed to wander back to the old castle, mourning over the chest of gold, until somebody shall follow her to the mysterious vault where it lies buried, remove it, and thus give her unquiet spirit rest.

During the eighteenth century there lived in two of the barely habitable rooms of the then neglected and crumbling castle, a labourer of the estate and his family. Both rooms must have served as bedrooms, because one night the parents were roused from their sleep by loud screams coming from the next room. Rushing in, they found their boy sitting up in bed, trembling, soaked in sweat, evidently in extreme terror.

"The White Lady! the White Lady!" screamed the boy, covering his eyes with his hands.

"What lady?" cried his mother, staring round the empty room. "There is no lady here."

"She is gone," the child whimpered, "but she looked so angry at me because I wouldn't go with her. She looked a fine lady—she sat down by my bed and wrung her hands and she cried and cried—and then she kissed me and asked me to go with her—she said she would make me a very rich man, as she had buried a big box of gold, hundreds of years ago, down in the vault, and she wanted to give it me because she could not rest while it was there. When I said I was afraid to go, she tried to carry me off and lifted me up, and then I shrieked and frightened her away."

The parents felt full of fear and astonishment. They knew the castle was supposed to be haunted by a white lady, but up to now they had been undisturbed. Neither of them had seen or heard anything. Telling themselves that the child must have been dreaming, they managed to soothe and quiet him and they eventually got him to sleep. But the same thing happened on the three succeeding nights, there being little variation each time in the child's story. Then they moved him out of the castle, and heard no more of the spectre. The boy never dared to enter the old castle alone, not even in daylight. As a man he persisted in the truth of what he had seen and told; at forty years old he had only to recall the scene to shudder, feeling again the Lady's cold lips on his cheeks, the clammy embrace of her clinging bloodless arms. This man became a settler in Canada and was alive in 1805.

Belief in the treasure at Blenkinsopp Castle was strengthened about the middle of the nineteenth century by the arrival of a strange lady at the adjacent village. She had dreamt that a large chest of gold lay buried in the castle vaults; what is more, when she first arrived she at once recognised the castle as the one she had seen in her dream—perhaps an example of precognition or clairvoyance. She stayed at the inn a few weeks, awaiting the return of the owner of the castle to ask leave to search. But the reason for her pilgrimage to Blenkinsopp was betrayed by her hostess, and the lady departed, possibly from a dislike of publicity, without achieving her search.

Up until 1820 various poor families continued to live in the ancient castle, which remained badly neglected and ruinous. Later on, the owner of a neighbouring farm ordered the vaults to be cleared out so that he could winter his cattle in them. While this was being done, a small doorway, level with the bottom of the keep, was found. The place smelt damp and foul. News quickly spread that the entrance to the "Lady's Vault" had been discovered, and people flocked to see it. Only one man, however, was willing to enter the narrow passage not high enough to allow him to walk upright. He groped forward a few yards, descended some steps, went forward again until he reached a doorway half fallen to pieces, the door rotting, the bolt rusted up, hinges hanging. Here the passage took a sudden turn and he made out a flight of steps leading steeply downwards. Peering over his lantern, he saw what appeared a long distance down into darkness; but noxious gases extinguished his light and he was forced to stumble blindly back to his companions. He made one more attempt, but he never descended the second flight of stairs. His employer ordered the entrance to be sealed up and the contents of the vault has remained undiscovered to this day.

Blenkinsopp Castle was restored and renovated later in the nineteenth century, and for a time was owned by a Colonel Coulson. Then, during the 'nineties, it was rented by the Anne family; and, as I have already mentioned, Major George Anne's father saw the famous White Lady, in 1893. Major Ernest Anne was going to Iceland, and had come up from London by train to collect his belongings, being under the impression that the castle was empty except for two servant girls. He was in the hall and was just about to go upstairs when he noticed a woman in a white dress leaning on the banisters; she seemed to be gazing at him with a piercing look. He thought it must be one of the maids; so, instead of going on upstairs, he decided to take a short walk in the garden. He found *both* the servants picking vegetables in the kitchen-garden. The house was empty.

Major Ernest Anne's youngest son, Bob, who was killed in action in 1917, was born at Blenkinsopp, and when he was little more than two years old is said to have seen the ghost. Apparently, he was heard, through the night-nursery door, to shout the words "Go away, lady!" While one must readily admit that a child of two can hardly be quoted as an authority, it is nevertheless true that some young children are extra sensitive to psychic phenomena. Major George Anne told me that in those early days other things used to happen at Blenkinsopp Castle: violent knocks would be heard on the bedroom door, always at 2 a.m. and 5 a.m., so regularly that it was possible to set a watch by them; sometimes the paraffin lamp would be alarmingly turned off as one lay in bed reading.

That Bamburgh Castle was haunted within living memory I have evidence from a reliable personal source. When I was motoring through the West Country on a "ghost-hunting" expedition, I had the pleasure of being entertained to tea by Miss Sylvia Calmady-Hamlyn at Buckfastleigh. Miss Calmady-Hamlyn is an elderly lady of charm, wit, and altogether forceful character, who has many different interests. Her mastery of the practical side of life may be inferred by the quite authoritative position she has won in breeding Dartmoor ponies, as well as by the fact that she has long been a Chief Magistrate in Devonshire.

The conversation had turned to the occult. Miss Calmady-Hamlyn said: "It's stupid ignorance and nonsense not to believe in ghosts! Just plumb stupid. Listen, I was born in 1881. About the years 1898 to 1900 I was living in rooms in the twelfth-century Norman keep of Bamburgh Castle, which at that time was the home of my cousins. You can work out my age for yourself. As a girl in my 'teens I both saw and heard a ghost in my bedroom in the keep. He came across the floor of the room about midnight, filmy grey, and he sounded to be clanking chains. Only when he left and walked outside my room did his boots clank loudly down the three-foot passage and then down the steps—all stone of course."

Berry Pomeroy Castle, in its seclusion about two and a half miles from Totnes by an uphill road, is the most picturesque of the Devonshire castles. Today it is a romantically beautiful ruin, almost buried in deep woods on the edge of a steep cliff, round the bottom of which winds a tributary of the river Dart. Some of the beech trees must be nearly as old as much of Berry Castle itself, described as "perhaps the most ivy-covered of all ruins in Southern England." And in this spot, at an unknown date, a terrible tragedy is reputed to have taken place.

Berry Pomeroy has been owned by only two families since the Norman Conquest—the Pomeroys (the great Norman family of de la Pomerai owned it from 1066 until 1548) and the Seymours. An Edwardian castle was built on the site of a medieval manor house by one of the Pomeroys in the early fourteenth century, and of this original stronghold the most notable present-day survival is the ivy-clad gatehouse, with its massive curtain-wall, leading into a courtyard in which are the ruins of the Tudor mansion begun, most likely, by the Lord Protector's son, who lived here from 1575 until his death in 1593. The Seymours continued to live at Berry for most of the seventeenth century.

A little wild fact, other than legend, is preserved about the Pomeroys. The late Sir Charles Oman, K.B.E., of All Souls College, who was Chichele Professor of Modern History at Oxford, has written in his book, *Castles*: "The Pomeroys were among the most powerful of the early Devonian feudal houses, and had the unusual luck of continuing their lineal succession for nearly 500 years, during which they never lost their lands for a permanence, though they were more than once in danger of confiscation for treason. Henry de Pomeroy was a resolute supporter of John Lackland in his rebellion against Richard I, and when forced to fly from Berry seized the impregnable Cornish rock of Mount St. Michael, and held it till all hope was gone. It would appear that he escaped forfeiture by committing suicide; having assigned his lands to his sons, he had himself bled to death by his surgeon, in the ancient Roman fashion. And Richard I, since he had never been tried or condemned, allowed the Pomeroy lands to escape confiscation. The local legend at Berry—quite unauthentic—gives Henry a still more lurid end—he is said to have blindfolded his horse, and then to have ridden him out of the postern straight down the precipitous north side of the castle, ending with a broken neck in the ravine below."

Of the Seymours Sir Charles Oman tells us: "It was the earliest of the Seymour owners of Berry who cleared out part of the interior of the old castle of the Pomeroys in order to erect in the centre of the walls that magnificent Tudor building whose ruins strike the eye of the visitor so much more effectively than the ivy-smothered remnants of the old *enceinte*. It is one of those mansions built for light and convenience, with enormous mullioned windows, which occupy more than half of its frontage, and with long galleries and spacious reception rooms, in which the period 1550–1600 is so rich. Apparently the interior decorations were elaborate almost to ostentation, mantelpieces of polished marble instead of freestone, fluted Corinthian pillars, cornices of wreathed fruit and flowers highly gilt, ceilings of curiously figured plaster, panelling of precious woods; the building is said to have cost £20,000—a great sum in Tudor days. "Yet the whole was never brought to completion, for the west side was never begun," says the author of the *Worthies of Devon*, himself an eighteenth-century vicar of Berry.

"Here lived five generations of Seymours, knights and afterwards baronets, prominent among the noble families of Devon. But the great Civil War brought harm to Berry, as to so many other ancient castles; the walls were 'slighted,' and the residence somewhat damaged. It must still have been habitable in 1688, as Sir Edward Seymour brought William of Orange thither on his march from Torbay to Newton Abbot.... Tradition says that the roofs of Berry were fired by lightning in a storm, and that the owner, considering it a rather remote, if splendid, abode, would not go to the expense of reconstruction. Two hundred years of wind and rain have done the rest, and the once magnificent building is a picturesque skeleton, showing the sky through scores of mullioned ribs."

Against such a history and background, we have the story of an uncouth event. We do not know the date, but we may presume that it was early. We are, at least, on historic ground in writing of Dr. Walter Farquhar, who was born in 1738 and died in 1819. Sir Walter Farquhar, as he later became, being created a baronet on the first of March, 1796, was soon afterwards appointed physician in ordinary to the Prince of Wales, and numbered among his patients many persons of rank and influence. He was, it seems, a man of the highest personal character, noted for his probity and veracity, whose skill in his profession inspired the greatest confidence and made him the favourite physician, even the personal friend, of the Prince Regent. His portrait was painted by Sir Henry Raeburn, who painted portraits of a large number of his distinguished contemporaries. Sir Walter Farquhar became one of the highest authorities in the medical world.

One day, towards the end of the eighteenth century, while Dr. Farquhar was staying at Torquay, he was called professionally to Berry Pomeroy Castle, a part of which was still occupied by a steward and his wife. The wife was seriously ill, and it was to see her that he had been called in. Dr. Farquhar was shown into a large, badly proportioned apartment, which was panelled in richly carved black oak. The only light in the room filtered through the chequered panes of a gorgeous stained-glass window emblazoned with the arms of the former lords of Berry Pomeroy. There was a wide fireplace, and in one corner—says the narrative attributed to the doctor—dark oaken steps formed part of a staircase leading to some room above; these stairs were touched by the last gleams of a summer's twilight.

While Dr. Farquhar perhaps just wondered, or chafed, at the imposed delay that kept him from his patient, the door opened and a young woman, somewhat richly dressed, entered the apartment. Supposing her to be one of the family, Dr. Farquhar moved forward to meet her. Ignoring him, she crossed the room with a hasty step, wringing her hands, and showing signs of the deepest anguish. She paused for an instant at the foot of the stairs, then began to climb them hurriedly and in great agitation. When she reached the highest stair the light fell strongly on her features and showed a countenance, young indeed and beautiful; but it was a face in which lust and despair fought for mastery. "If ever human face," to use the doctor's own words, "exhibited agony and remorse; if ever eye, that index of the soul, portrayed anguish uncheered by hope, and suffering without interval; if ever features betrayed that within the wearer's bosom there dwelt a hell, those features and that being were then presented to me."

Brooding upon this strange phenomenon, Dr. Farquhar was summoned to the bedside of his patient. He found the lady so ill that he had neither the opportunity nor the wish to ask questions outside the subject of her illness. But the next morning she seemed better, and he at once told her husband what he had witnessed and asked if there was any explanation. The steward's face had fallen; and, when the doctor had finished, he cried:

"My poor wife! My poor wife!"

"Why, how does what I have seen affect her?"

"That it should have come to this!" replied the steward with distracted vehemence. "I can't—can't lose her! You don't know," he said in a wild tone, "the strange, awful story—and his lordship is extremely against any allusion ever being made to the tale or any importance being attached to it—but I must and will tell you! You have seen the ghost of the daughter of a former baron of Berry Pomeroy, who bore a child to her own father. In that room above us the fruit of their wicked incestuous intercourse was strangled by the guilty mother. Now, whenever death is about to come to anybody in the castle, the crazed phantom is seen hurrying to the scene of her crime, with the frenzy you describe. When my son was drowned she was seen—now it is my wife!"

"But your wife is better. All immediate danger is over."

"No," said the steward, "I have lived by the castle thirty years. The omen never fails."

"Absurd to argue about omens," answered the doctor. "I trust to see your wife recovered."

They parted in disagreement. The lady died at noon.

Many years went by. When Sir Walter Farquhar was at the zenith of his professional career, a lady called on him for a consultation about her sister, whom she described as sinking, utterly heart-broken and overcome by a supernatural apparition she swore she had seen. One morning, the lady explained, they had driven over from Torquay to visit the fine ruins of Berry Pomeroy Castle. The steward was ill at the time—in fact he died as they were going over the ruins—and while the lady and her brother went off in search of the keys, the sister was left alone in a large room on the ground-floor. They returned with the keys to find her in a state almost of collapse, muttering excitedly about a female spectre she had seen, whose contorted features and appearance of indescribable distress would never fade from her mind. "I know," the lady told Sir Walter, "that you will say all this is quite preposterous, and indeed we have tried to treat the matter with scorn and to laugh my sister out of it. But when we joke, she only grows more agitated. Will you please see her without delay?"

"I will, immediately," replied the eminent doctor, "but I must tell you, before I attend your sister, that this is no delusion. I myself have seen the same figure in somewhat similar circumstances and at about the same time of the day. Believe me, it is no joking matter."

Sir Walter saw the young lady next day, and after a short treatment under his care she recovered.

I have adapted and slightly modernised this story from *The Haunted Homes and Family Traditions Of Great Britain* by

John H. Ingram, which was first published in 1884. John Ingram claims that the account of how Berry Pomeroy Castle is haunted has been told as nearly as possible in Sir Walter Farquhar's own words.

A number of other castles in Britain have the persistent reputation of being haunted, best known great "Glamis itself, the most picturesque building in Scotland, girdled with pepper-box turrets," with its weird chamber where King Duncan was murdered by Macbeth, and somewhere in the lost depths of its walls "another chamber more ghastly still, with a secret, transmitted from the fourteenth century, which is always known to three persons"; and Powis Castle in Wales; but these castles are perhaps outside the scope of this book. Then there are Corby Castle in Cumberland, Hilton and Lambton Castles in Durham, and Peele and Rushen Castles in the Isle of Man, all with strange legends to be found in John Ingram's illustrated volume, in Charles Harper's *Haunted Houses*, or in Mrs. Catherine Crowe's much earlier (1848), old-fashioned but valuable *The Night Side of Nature*.

Yet there is one more castle of which, as one who lives not far from it, I feel drawn to give some account, and that is Herstmonceux Castle in Sussex. The building of this moated, now warmly mellowed, brick castle was begun in 1440 by Sir Roger de Fiennes, who fought at Agincourt, on the site of an older mansion; and the bricks used, and probably also the bricklayers, were Flemish, because brick buildings were little known so early in England. There is an avenue of twisted Spanish chestnuts that is mentioned in the old books. Herstmonceux Castle, today restored from almost complete ruin and neglect to perhaps more than its ancient beauty, was a private residence until 1946 when it was sold to the Admiralty and became the home of the Royal Observatory; as Mr. Reginald Turnor has written, it "has a fitting serenity in which to contemplate the stars."

But the restoration is only recent, started in 1910 when Colonel Claude Lowther bought it from Squire Curtis. As Mrs. Esther Meynell points out in her book *Sussex*, "for long all this lovely brickwork was smothered in great swags of clutching and destroying ivy. Prints of a century ago show every architectural grace hidden by this poisonous plant... it had battlemented walls, machicolated towers, a draw-bridge, portcullis and moat. The entrance gateway, with its massive flanking towers, is a noble piece of work, and the workmanship, and the warm peach-red of the bricks make a lovely picture in the Sussex landscape. And all this beauty was smothered under a cloak of ivy for years, till the castle gateway looked like a crouching old crone."

Many ghosts have been rumoured to haunt the romantic precincts of Herstmonceux Castle; but I have talked with Mr. W. N. Parker, who has worked there as a gardener since the first years of this century; yet he could give me no corroboration of the more recent tales. It has been said that Colonel Claude Lowther, who lived in the castle in 1910, once met a girl in the courtyard, who was wringing white and shrivelled hands. Supposing her to be some vagrant gipsy in trouble, he spoke to her when she instantly vanished. On another occasion a somnambulistic-looking male phantom is reported to have stumbled straight against, and right through, the mettlesome horse which Colonel Lowther was riding. Then there is the better-known legend of the phantom drummer of Herstmonceux, the ghost apparently of a giant drummer, nine feet high, who served in the guard of Sir Roger de Fiennes who built the castle in 1440, and was believed to walk the battlements outside Drummer's Hall producing the paranormal beating of a drum. Another version of this happening has been given by Augustus Hare: "It is said that a Lord Dacre, who was supposed to be dead, long lived here in concealment, and beat a mysterious drum to frighten away the suitors of his widow when they appeared." Or again, the ghostly drummer may well have found his origin in the past, widespread practice of smuggling. Heard, or seen, by petrified rustics when they were occasionally obliged to walk near the ruined castle at night, the "drummer" may have been a confederate of the Hastings and Eastbourne gang of smugglers, who used the then roofless walls of the castle, and the "altar-tombs" of the adjoining churchyard, as store-houses. All the smuggler would need to do would be to rub a little phosphorus on his face

Herstmonceux Castle, Sussex.

and parade the spot once in a while with his drum, wearing an ancient uniform, and the place would be shunned. Spirits—if not ghosts—certainly issued from those altar-tombs!

The Story of My Life by Augustus Hare is a spacious, and in parts extremely interesting, book, which contains a number of good ghost stories. It was written in six volumes during the reign of Queen Victoria, when people had leisure for such bounty. Its opening paragraph gives a sinister report relating to Herstmonceux: "In 1727, the year of George the First's death, Miss Grace Naylor of Hurstmonceaux, though she was beloved, charming, and beautiful, died very mysteriously in her twenty-first year, in the immense and weird old castle of which she had been the heiress. She was affirmed to have been starved by her former governess, who lived alone with her, but the fact was never proved." This cruel murder is reputed to have happened in a room known as the Lady's Bower, but neither the power nor the motive of the governess have ever been explained.

The reason that the great castle ever fell into complete ruin was the traditional jealousy and greed of a stepmother. During the eighteenth century Herstmonceux Castle had come into the possession of the Hares, and a Robert Hare, who was made a Canon of Winchester, had married while still very young a beautiful heiress, Sarah Selman. Augustus Hare shall tell the story. "In the zenith of her youth and loveliness, however, Sarah Hare died very suddenly from eating ices when overheated at a ball, and soon afterwards Robert married a second wife—the rich Henrietta Henckel, who pulled down Hurstmonceaux Castle. She did this because she was jealous of the sons of her predecessor, and wished to build a large new house, which she persuaded her husband to settle upon her own children, who were numerous, though only two daughters lived to any great age. But she was justly punished, for when Robert Hare died, it was discovered that the great house which Wyatt had built for Mrs. Hare, and which is now known as Hurstmonceaux Place, was erected upon entailed land, so that the house stripped of furniture, and the property shorn of its most valuable farms, passed to Francis Hare-Naylor, son of Miss Selman. Mrs. Henckel Hare lived on to a great age, and when 'the burden of her years came on her' she repented of her avarice and injustice, and coming back to Hurstmonceaux in childish senility, would wander round and round the castle ruins in the early morning and late evening, wringing her hands and saying—'Who could have done such a wicked thing: oh! who could have done such a wicked thing, as to pull down this beautiful old place?' Then her daughters, Caroline and Marianne, walking beside her, would say—'Oh dear mamma, it was you who did it, it was you yourself who did it, you know'—and she would despairingly resume—'Oh no, that is impossible: it could not have been me. I could not have done such a wicked thing: it could not have been me that did it.' My cousin Marcus Hare had at Abbots Kerswell a picture of Mrs. Henckel Hare, which was always surrounded with crape bows."

And now we come to the last of the stories about Herstmonceux, again fully recorded by Augustus Hare in his massive autobiography, which sounds to me like an authentic ghost story. A George Hare, who was born in 1781, grew up and went to India, from which country he wrote home regularly and prosperously to his family. After a time his relations heard that he had died. They had always thought him very rich, but on his death no money was forthcoming. Those on the spot wrote that he had left no money, and his relations began to wonder whether the report of his death itself could be fictitious. India, in those far off days, seemed impossibly remote and inaccessible, and the whole subject was gradually allowed to drop.

Telling it as a strange story of later days, Augustus Hare writes: "It was some time after our great family misfortunes in 1859... that I chanced to pass through London, where I saw my eldest brother, Francis, who asked me if we had any ancestor or relation who had gone to India and had died there. I said 'No', for at that time I had never heard of George Hare or of the Bishop's youngest son, Francis, who likewise died in India. But my brother insisted that we must have had an Indian relation who died there; and on my inquiring 'why,' he told me the following story. He assured me, that being resolved once more to visit the old family home, he had gone down to Hurstmonceaux, and had determined to pass the night in the castle. That in the high tower by the gateway he had fallen asleep, and that in a vision he had seen an extraordinary figure attired in the dress of the end of the last century and with a pig-tail, who assured him that he was a near relation of his, and was come to tell him that though he was supposed to have died in India and insolvent, he had really died very rich, and that if his relations chose to make inquiries, they might inherit his fortune! At the time I declared that the story could not be true, as we never had any relation who had anything to do with India, but Francis persisted steadfastly in affirming what he had seen and heard, and some time afterwards I was told of the existence of George Hare." I have not heard that the fortune ever turned up.

So we must leave haunted castles in general, and Herstmonceux in particular with all its modern instruments, its giant telescopic lenses cocked at the riddle of the stars; holding the secrets of the past, but more than ever a challenge of enduring beauty with its quiet dignity of restored rose-red brickwork and windows giving views across the long flat hazy green reaches of the levels to the faint blue distant downs.

Chapter Four

A West Country Ghost-Hunt

ACCORDING to Mr. Geoffrey Gorer, many of the findings in whose book *Exploring English Character* are based upon an inquiry covering the whole of the English population and the analysis of 5,000 questionnaires, a sixth of the population believe in ghosts and just under a quarter have not made up their minds. "There are two men to three women among the believers in ghosts (13 per cent and 21 per cent); the uncertain are nearly evenly divided; the disbelievers have some 10 per cent more men than women." A sixth of the population own mascots, or owned them in war-time. Incidentally, it is only in the holding of war-time mascots, which amount to private pieces of solid magic, that most of the men in the English working-class show themselves more believing than their womenfolk. And, we are told, about one serving man in three had a mascot.

Now mascots may be silly—whether such religious symbols as a plain cross or a St. Christopher come into the category of mascots I am uncertain—but I would remind those of a confirmed sceptical turn of mind, who may already perhaps be feeling scornful, that the world's no doubt greatest living psychologist,

Dr. Carl Jung, has been glad to admit in a recent interview that "over the nearly 60 years he has practised and developed his vast knowledge of the human mind, he has grown to realise that there are some things that cannot be explained by normal or earthly factors."

I have always known that the West Country is a haunted land. It should be remembered that West Country people are not uncompromisingly matter-of-fact, nor obstinately cynical. Whether they call them wraiths, phantoms, spirits, apparitions, poltergeists, goblins, knackers or piskies, many West Country people believe in ghosts and the stories they tell are certainly true in the sense that the tellers themselves are convinced that the supernormal events happened. Anyhow, the whole literature of ghosts is far too extensive to be treated lightly, and we may come to the conclusion that some chilling descriptions are founded upon well-attested facts. In the face of circumstantial evidence, the sneer, or laugh, of the scoffer may often quite likely be but a symptom of doubt or unease. As Dr. Johnson said of the belief in ghosts: "All argument is against it, but all belief is for it."

So in April, 1955, taking advantage of a rare warm spell of fine weather, I motored down into the West Country to see what I could find out. My first destination and investigation was at Wookey Hole in Somerset, where I was fortunate in knowing Mrs. Olive Hodgkinson, the beautiful wife of Wing Commander G. W. Hodgkinson, the present owner of Wookey Hole, whose family has owned the caves for generations. Some short account of the caves must be given, because of their slight connexion with what follows.

At Wookey we are in a legend-haunted countryside. The series of underground caverns at the foot of the Mendip Hills are only two miles from the little, perfect cathedral city of Wells which, like Matthew Arnold's Oxford, is still today whispering the last enchantments of the Middle Age; and eight miles from mystic Glastonbury, with its legends of Joseph of Arimathea and the tombs of Arthur and Guinevere and its identification with Avalon. The caves are near the landlocked "isle" of Athelney, where Alfred is supposed to have burnt the cakes, and not far from the flat expanses of King's Sedgmoor, where still, they say, tattered fugitives from Monmouth's defeated rebellion are seen, as ghosts, fleeing across the marshes—phantoms of the soldiers hanged by Judge Jeffreys.

Wookey Hole, with its high, hollow, macabre caverns and slow, subterranean, jade River Axe, is the oldest known home of man in Great Britain and was inhabited alternately by humans and ancient kinds of wild animal from 60,000 to 100,000 years ago. And long before that huge white stalagmites had dripped away aeons of Time.

Numerous excavations of the floors of the interconnecting caves have proved that in later times Celtic tribes (the Ancient Britons) found refuge in Wookey Hole: from about 250 B.C. until the Romans left round A.D. 450 they were allowed to live in peace. Afterwards, the invading Saxons gradually drove them back into Cornwall and Wales.

The first chamber the visitor is shown is known as the Witch's Kitchen, and the legend belonging to this cavern provides the sinister side of Wookey. A baleful black stalagmite formation, dominating the mysterious river, clearly depicts the menacing nutcracker profile of an old witch woman. The legend of the "Witch of Wookey" has been passed from father to son in the village for a thousand years: it tells of an evil woman who long ago lived in the cave with her goats, casting blasting spells on happy lovers, farmers' cattle and crops, until for her wickedness she was turned into stone, a warning image of just retribution, by a monk from Glastonbury.

That is the legend. But the facts are, to say the least, remarkable. During some excavations carried out in 1912, there were unearthed from a depth of ten feet, about forty yards inside the cave, the skeleton of a youngish woman, together with a dagger, a sacrificial knife, a milking pot, a weaving comb and a ball of milk-white stalagmite that resembled a witch's crystal. And close by were found the bones of two goats around the stake to which they must have once been tethered! These objects are in the museum at Wells. From skulls and other bones of the late Celtic period salvaged from the river, we may be almost certain that human blood once flowed here, that human sacrifice was practised.

Mrs. Olive Hodgkinson had not long returned from a successful visit to the United States and Canada, where she had broadcast and televised on Wookey Caves and the ghost I had come to hear about. She told me over luncheon that she had been advertised in the States as "England's Cave Woman!"—absurdly hard to credit when face to face with her beauty and attractive sophistication. The haunted house, which I saw with her in the afternoon, was on the Wookey estate, one of some cottages built about 1878.

"It was most extraordinary," Mrs. Hodgkinson explained. "About eight years ago—yes, I think she died in 1947—one of our vintage tenants, a perfectly normal old lady who had lived in this cottage for sixty years, died a perfectly natural death, aged eighty odd. We had more than once tried to put electricity into the cottage, but she had always bitterly opposed this scheme, she didn't like these new-fangled ideas! Well, after she died we had the electricity put in, but her husband and son left. Some new people came in temporarily, while waiting for their own house to be built. The old lady had originally been the bride of an operative in a paper mill; but the cottage was one we now intended to use for staff cottages. The new couple had a small boy of eight years old, and one evening he went upstairs and came down looking very frightened. 'Who's the old lady upstairs, Mummy?' he asked. The mother at once took him upstairs to investigate—she saw the ghost of the old lady walking across this landing. The family just couldn't stand it, they complained that they saw the ghost so often and heard footsteps coming both up and down stairs. They went. Now we found we couldn't let the cottage either furnished or unfurnished, because of the ghost, footsteps, and doors opening and shutting."

Mrs. Hodgkinson and I were talking on the landing. We had come out of the quite simple, plainly furnished bedroom.

"The Institute of Psychical Research," Mrs. Hodgkinson went on, "sent an investigator down and she and I sat up one whole night in the cottage, but we saw nothing. As you know, our garden leads up to the cave entrance: our cats and dogs would always come with us and even enter the mouth of the cave, but none of them would ever pass the effigy of the Witch of Wookey! Thinking that the ghost might possibly have some odd connexion with the Witch, I had taken the two cats with us into the haunted cottage to watch their behaviour. One of them curled round and fell asleep in a chair quite naturally; but the other one, the old black cat Tabitha, was terrified and sat awake all night, she never closed her eyes all night long. Exactly at 5 a.m. both the investigator and I thought we heard something move, although by that time it may have been imagination.... The funny thing was that the cat which had until then been sound asleep, suddenly at that very moment sprang out of the chair and leapt on to the window-ledge, while Tabitha shot away up the stairs all her hackles rising!"

"Queer," I said.

"Another thing," said Mrs. Hodgkinson, "our manageress at the time was very sceptical and thought the whole business was absolute nonsense; though she was too polite to say so, of course. She agreed to sleep in the haunted cottage, but from the first minute she experienced an extraordinary feeling and she couldn't sleep. She got up and went and fetched the assistant manageress, persuading her to go through the cottage with her. Of course they found nothing unusual. Then about 2 a.m. the manageress felt a cold hand upon her shoulder; starting up in terror from her bed, she saw the ghost of a female figure walking through the doorway. Next morning she told me she knew precisely what it meant to say a person's hair was standing on end; and when I first saw her I thought her own hair still was standing on end. She was white and looking completely shattered."

At the time of my visit the chef at Wookey had just insisted on changing his bedroom in the cottage because he had been sleepless, most unhappy and ill at ease in the haunted bedroom. Another horrible symptom complained of by all who had had anything to do with the haunted cottage when the ghost was about, was a hideous cold, almost fungoid, dead smell which, it was insisted, you could not mistake for anything natural. The cottage, I understand, was blessed, with a reading of prayers, by the Rev. Christopher Leach, the Vicar of Wookey, in 1954, in an attempt to lay the ghost.

Miss Calmady-Hamlyn, who lives within little more than a stone's throw from Buckfast Abbey in South Devonshire, told me she believes that the Manor House at North Huish (now North Huish Rectory) was haunted as late as the first quarter of our century by the ghost of a bearded and brown-habited Cistercian monk. Her belief relies upon the first hand testimony of her close friend, Mrs. Verner-Jeffreys, who rented the Manor House for fourteen years, from mid-June, 1914 until June, 1928. Miss Calmady-Hamlyn considers that the Manor was once a grange of the old Abbey, where much busy farming would have been done; but that a curse came upon the house after the Monasteries were dissolved by Henry VIII in 1539.

Another ghost story concerns the Benedictine Buckfast Abbey. In 1872 or 1873 a boy of twelve was alone fishing in the pool of the river Dart facing the site of the ancient Abbey. He was setting his bait when he thought he heard a rustling of leaves and branches. Looking round, he saw a number of monks walking in Indian file and in perfect silence. They wore white habits, and slowly disappeared from his view. The boy was so excited by the success he was having at fishing, that it never occurred to him to mention what he had seen until many years afterwards. The odd thing is that this apparition manifested itself ten years before the Benedictine monks returned to Buckfast.

Mrs. Verner-Jeffreys's husband, Commander Verner-Jeffreys, R.N. (a descendant of Judge Jeffreys) was tragically lost off the Faroes in February, 1915, when H.M.S. *Clan McNaughton* went down with all hands. A son was born to Mrs. Verner-Jeffreys six weeks after his father's death. This boy was the only one of the family to see the ghost of the Cistercian monk. He was five years old, Mrs. Verner-Jeffreys told me, and slept in a night-nursery in the oldest and least pleasant wing of the house, which overlooked a churchyard. One night he informed his mother: "I've had a funny old man sitting on my bed. He was like

Buckfast Abbey. "Looking round, he saw a number of monks walking in Indian file and in perfect silence."

Father Christmas." Questioned further, the child spoke of a gown and a beard, but wasn't at all afraid. "On the other hand," Mrs. Verner-Jeffreys avers, "none of my adult friends liked to walk up the drive after dusk—they were afraid to! Then doors flew open and bells suddenly rang. There were terrifying noises. People said it was rats, but it wasn't I can promise you. The house could be decidedly unpleasant. I know that the Monk's Walk was haunted, because I once saw a hooded brown figure in the Archway. The curse on the house was true. My son was killed in the Second World War. But it is likely that the Manor House has survived the long spell of cursing and is now a happy house again."

Miss Calmady-Hamlyn has every reason to believe in the cruel power of cursing and of witchcraft, because her own father died of it while still a comparatively young man near his home at Bridestowe, North Devon, in the year 1897. I have taken the following account of this extraordinary event from an article, *Three Lifton Magistrates Died—By Witchcraft?* by Sylvia Calmady-Hamlyn, contributed to the *Western Morning News*, Plymouth, on June 25th, 1953:

"My father, Vincent Waldo Calmady-Hamlyn, was the third son of Shilston Calmady, of Leawood and Paschoe, and had made his own way in the world when he unexpectedly inherited the family homes. He was a scholar of Balliol—in the famous days of Jowett—a Prize Essayman and history first and then a barrister at Lincoln's Inn. He also wrote regularly for the *Pall Mall*, the *Spectator*, and the *Anti-Jacobin*.

"His interests being in London, he only came to Leawood for the three summer months, where his step-mother joined us to keep house. I was about ten when we first went there and I rode my Dartmoor pony a good deal alone about the district. My father made me promise never to go on a certain rather poor little farm, lying under the Moor, and naturally I never did. He told me once that there were bad people called black witches, who did harm to their neighbours, but that quite harmless old women often got that reputation unjustly and that he and I were going to take soup to one such victim, living in great poverty and isolation, because the villagers refused to allow her to come to the village. And this we often did.

"On September 1, 1897, we rode, as was his custom, to Lifton Court, the other two magistrates being Mr. Kelly of Kelly and a man whose name I forget. The noted black witch had been summoned for the first time by the police for some offence of theft and the magistrates gave her a nominal fine, my father, I think, being in the chair. As they left the courthouse, the witch stood on the steps and cursed them, giving my father at most three days to live, Mr. Kelly two years, and the third man three years. Of course Bridestowe village rang that night with the news of the cursing of the magistrates, particularly of 'Squire'.

"On September 2, my father went out riding about 10.30 a.m., while I was still at lessons. At noon, a frightened tenant came with news of 'an accident to Squire,' and we waited. At three o'clock the Rector came and told us that my father had been found dead, with his horse standing by, at a spot not far from the black witch's holding. He was forty-four years old. Within a week, I was back again at my grandfather's home in Yorkshire, 'an orphan and a ward' until I was twenty-one, and Leawood passed to another.

"Within two years I was visiting my step-grandmother at Exmouth, where she lived, and saw a paralysed, helpless man in a bath chair—Mr. Kelly of Kelly, who shortly died. The third magistrate died within the limit of his curse.

"I did not know the story until, at twenty-one, I returned to Bridestowe to a tiny home of my own when the Rector there told it to me, and added: 'I have preached against the power of witchcraft all my time, but after that it was no longer any good.'"

There is an authentic coda to this terrible tale of cursing by the Black Witch of Bridestowe, less drastic, but still malicious and evil. The present blacksmith at Ashburton, who had been a Bridestowe lad, recently and quite casually while doing a pony, told Miss Calmady-Hamlyn something she had never heard. Apparently, a hard-bitten farmer, who acted as bailiff for her father, went to warn the witch about one of her harmful activities and she threatened him: "You keep off, John Lintern, or it will be the worse for you." He replied: "You can't frighten me, I am too stout a fellow." The witch said: "All right, then I'll get at you through one of yours." When the farmer got home he found his wife in agony—she had upset the scalding cream all over her.

Though today some of us may suspect that Time is a cheat, it will make for variety if we continue to journey backwards and forwards in our earthly time to find our ghosts. Whether to an earth-bound ghost our time is nothing, or infernally long, we have no means of knowing. But from talking with those who have confronted a supernormal phantasm, a visitation, where the laws of fact, of probability, and of time itself are transcended, I get the impression that the overwhelming, alarming upset which they feel springs first from a sense that they have lost their bearings. The normal is flatly contradicted, nay confounded. . . . More than ever at this moment of history we need to believe in miracles, all of which, Carlyle reminds us, have been wrought by thought. Also the French have a proverb to the effect that "there are no miracles for those who have no faith in them."

While we cannot establish the ghostly miracles of the past, where we are not in a position to cross-examine witnesses, some of these old tales have a rare period charm and seeming authenticity. I must here quote at some little length, because of its style as well as for its affiliation with Devonshire ghosts, Mrs. Bray, or rather, mostly, Mary Colling. In 1938 the house of John Murray republished, in three volumes, "TRADITIONS, LEGENDS, SUPERSTITIONS, AND SKETCHES *of* DEVONSHIRE *on the borders of* THE TAMAR AND THE TAVY, *Illustrative of its Manners, Customs, History, Antiquities, Scenery, and Natural History, In a Series of Letters to* ROBERT SOUTHEY, ESQ., *By Mrs. Bray.*" It is from Letter XXX that I will quote.

Vicarage, Tavistock,
January 8, 1833.

My dear Sir,
 I have heard Mary Colling (who is a most intelligent and exact registrar of all the old tales, traditions and characters of any note in her native town) tell etc. . . .

I was about to conclude this long "and very pithy" letter (as a good friend of mine calls the subjects on which I have been writing), when Mary Colling, who always acts as her own postman, brought me one written by herself, in reply to some questions I had proposed to her, about certain places, etc., in our town. I shall here, therefore, transcribe a portion of her letter, as it will give you a fair specimen of her prose style. Many are the authors and authoresses of this day who, from not being, like Mary content to follow nature, and to write as they would talk, produce a less pleasing mode of expression than the following.

"To Mrs. Bray.

"My dear Madam,
"On the south side of the Tavy is a hamlet consisting of several cottages, called in the parish register Dolvins, but better known to the inhabitants by the name of Guernsey, that nick-name having been given to it in consequence of a very noted smuggler who resided there some years ago. At a little distance eastward is another hamlet, called Greenland, from its cold situation; the sun seldom shines upon it, as it is overhung with a very high rock whence issue several springs of water; and during the winter the icicles (or, as the little boys call them, the cockables) which hang from it, are looked upon as a great curiosity, from their size and transparency. The Exeter road, opposite this hamlet, affords a picturesque view of the bright stream of water from the rock which dashes into your favourite Tavy. Near is a rookery and an orchard, that in summer adds to the beauty of the scene. The wild flowers, which there grow in abundance, have also a pretty appearance; and though the place is considered so cold, there is a very good garden that abounds with various sorts of flowers. The female who resides in a neat cottage attached to it, takes great pride in her garden, every corner of it having a something to boast of.

"In reply to the question about the haunted house, I have learned the following particulars. About half a mile from Tavistock there is a farm called Down House, the dwelling itself was rebuilt about eleven or twelve years ago. It was considered before an ancient place, and haunted by ghosts. Here is a story of one. The family who resided there well knew the hour of the night in which the ghosts made their appearance, and always took care to go to bed before it came. But it happened on a time that a child was very ill, and asked its mother for water; she went to the pitcher to get some, when the child refused any but such as might be got directly from the pump. The mother became quite distressed, unwilling to displease the child, yet afraid to go down to the pump, as it was about the hour in which the ghost walked. She considered upon it a little while, and the child still continuing very anxious about the water, she at last said, 'In the name of God I will go down.' She did so. Passing over the stairs she perceived a shadow, and then she heard footsteps; and when she came to the pump she felt a hand on her shoulder. She turned and perceived a tall man. Summoning a good resolution, however, she said, 'In the name of God, why troublest thou me?' The ghost replied, 'It is well for thee that thou hast spoken to me in the name of God; this being the last time allotted me to trouble this world, or else I should have injured thee. Now do as I tell thee, and be not afraid. Come with me and I will direct thee to a something which shall remove this pump: under it is concealed treasure.'

"This something was procured, and applied as the ghost directed. The pump was quickly removed, when under it there lay a great deal of money. She was desired to take up the treasure and stock her farm with it. And the spirit told her that if ever any person molested or deprived her of her property, he should suffer well for it. He then ordered her to go and give the water to the child, who, in reward for her courage and trust in God, should recover. The cock crew; directly the figure dwindled again to a shadow, ascended through the air, and she watched till he soon became a small bright cloud." ...

Thus ends Mary Colling's account, and my letter too, having sent quite enough hobgoblins for one packet; and lest the post-office should be troubled, and complain to Sir Francis Freeling if I send more, I will conclude with wishing you may be, my dear Sir, ghost-free all your days, saving from a few visits of Sir Thomas More, the renewal of whose "Colloquies" in the library of Keswick, would be a very desirable event for the public, and in which no individual of that body would feel a greater interest than your
Very gratefully obliged,
And most faithful servant,
Anna E. Bray.

Before we forsake the romantic spectres of the past in this part of the world, there is the legend of the wicked Monk of Haldon, a grim "six-century-old Christmas yarn" which was brought to my notice by Ruth Thomas, the lovely young journalist daughter of Gilbert Thomas, the poet. A serio-comic poem, "The Monk of Haldon," written in 1867 by a Rev. Barham who lived in Dawlish and was the son of Richard Harris Barham, the author of *The Ingoldsby Legends*, has done much to perpetuate interest in the tale; but the details of this poem are not history.

However, one Christmas Eve early in this century a man called Travers was walking home past the ruins of Lidwell Chapel along the main Haldon road from Teignmouth. The name Lidwell is commonly reputed to mean Our Lady's Well, and Travers was trying to discover the origin of the chapel. He told what happened to a friend over a glass of hot punch the same evening. "I was looking down into that corner, where, six months before, we had discovered the holy well. But the granite slab, which we had carefully replaced, had been thrust aside, and the black mouth of the well was exposed—but not completely! It was filled by the gasping, writhing head and shoulders of a man, hanging to the brink, while his feet and body were suspended over the blackness of the well. What I could see of him—or it—was clothed in the garment of a monk."

It is possible that Travers was romancing. He had malaria in his bones and one could easily attribute his story to a neurotic imagination. He would have heard the legend of the Haldon Phantom: how travellers carrying money used to disappear on the road from Teignmouth to Little Haldon. One night a sailor, going home from Plymouth to Exeter, at the invitation of the monk took shelter from a storm in the chapel. The sailor, perhaps drunk, foolishly admitted that he carried precious loot acquired through piracy. The monk fiercely denounced him. The sailor offered half his hoard in return for absolution. The appeased cleric inquired if he had been baptised. He had not; so the monk, placing both hands upon the sailor's shoulders, pushed him towards a crude font on the floor in the corner of the chancel. The sailor, who was evidently keen-witted and knew the world, became suspicious. He turned round just in time to see his confessor with a raised dagger ready to plunge into his back. There was a fight, but the sailor was sinewy, the stronger of the two, and at last flung the friar to the bottom of the well. Then the sailor knocked up a neighbouring peasant and told of his narrow escape over the embers of a fire in a cottage. Suspicion, of course, fell on the sailor; but with the first light of dawn the monk was recovered—alive—from the well, among the bones and rotting bodies of his other victims. The fate of the monk, if ever he existed, goes unrecorded.

Fact or fiction? We don't know, but perhaps Travers was not just imagining things after all. Many years before Lidwell Chapel was built a certain cleric, Robert de Middlecote, was accused and indicted, among other crimes, in the years 1328 and 1329 of "having maltreated with armed violence a certain Agnes, daughter of Roger, the miller, in the Chapel of the Blessed Virgin Mary on Walland Hill, Throwleigh, and of having killed her child"; and, as well as having committed many thefts, he was charged with the further crime of "robbing persons unknown on the highroad between Teignmouth and Haldon," which would bring him near Lidwell. Middlecote passed from history, but may have survived in the legend of the wicked monk who enticed travellers to Lidwell Chapel, murdered and robbed them and threw their bodies into the well.

"Time, which is the author of authors," as Francis Bacon so aptly comments, has assumed in our century the aura of a mystery. In *The New Immortality* J. W. Dunne writes: "Everything which has established its existence *remains in existence*. A rose which has bloomed once blooms for ever. As for Man, he is not accorded distinctive treatment; he merely remains with the rest." More and more today the S.P.R. is applying its methods of scientific experimentation to such matters as the new Time theories, precognition, and dreams of a future laid down in advance, with all forms of extra-sensory perception.

Now I was to cross the Tamar into the Duchy of Cornwall. Before leaving London my kindest Cornish friend, John Trewin, who so knowledgeably adorns with his books and dramatic criticism the lucky enchanted world of the theatre, had advised me to call upon Mr. W. H. Paynter in Liskeard. Mr. Paynter is a West Country authority on folklore, magic, witchcraft, ghosts, and kindred subjects. The Gorsedd of the Bards of Cornwall have conferred upon him the Cornish title of *Whyler Pystry*, which means "the searcher-out of witches," to honour his researches. Mr. Paynter I found as hospitable as he was interesting. We talked in his home until the small hours about all sorts of subjects, including Dunne's serial *"Time,"* when he gave me his own true account of a dream.

"It was a Friday night," Mr. Paynter told me, "I was living then at Callington. The next morning—on the Saturday—I had to go by bus to Truro. I dreamt I was in the bus, travelling along, when suddenly I saw out of the window in front a big black shape looming up. There was a crash—the sound of breaking glass. The bus stopped. I wasn't hurt, but in the dream I saw myself, quite distinctly, picking pieces of glass out of my clothes, where it had fallen down my chest. At breakfast I told my mother about the dream. She laughed and said: 'Oh, dear me, I hope nothing will happen like that!' I caught the bus and nothing happened till we came near Truro. Then I saw, just as in the dream, through the front window something big looming up. It was a stationary lorry loaded high with huge blocks of cement. The bus stopped. There seemed no room to pass. One of the lorry men was standing in the road, smoking, and beckoning to the bus driver. 'Come on, come on, mate,' he shouted, 'there's plenty of room to pass! You'll do it easy.' The driver looked very doubtful, but he was goaded into trying. Just as I thought we were clear, the bus felt suddenly to lurch. It jolted into the lorry. The glass in the window by me smashed, and there I was picking the broken pieces out of my clothes!" Surely a perfect example of a dream of the immediate future for Dunne's casebook.

While on the subject of possible visions into the future, Miss Daphne du Maurier in a delightful letter about her house, Menabilly, at Par in Cornwall, tells me of a story—late Victorian or even Edwardian—that a "lady in blue" was seen looking out of a bedroom window; but that she has never been able to trace who it was that actually saw this lady in blue. "It amuses me to imagine," writes Miss du Maurier, "that the lady in blue was not a phantom from the past, but a peep into the future. When I wrote *The King's General*, I wrote it in the room where the lady was supposed to appear, frequently looked out of the window for inspiration, and invariably wore a blue smock! So perhaps the Edwardian person walking across the lawn in 1910 had looked up and seen somebody of 1945 at the window!"

Of the many ghostly tales which my friend, *Whyler Pystry* of Liskeard, unfolded that evening I spent with him, I will choose two for their complete contrast, one pleasant, the other unpleasant. The first, "The Children and the Old Lady," happened in what must remain an anonymous West Country rectory.

The Rector and his wife were both gratified and puzzled because they had no difficulty—ever—in getting their two small children to bed. As soon as darkness approached the children would themselves suggest it was bedtime, and almost race each other to get there. One night as the puzzled parents passed the children's bedroom, they heard the younger child say: "I wonder if she'll come tonight?" The other one answered: "Of course she will if we are quiet."

The next evening, after hearing from the passage one child say: "She's come," the parents burst open the bedroom door.

"Oh, Mummy, Daddy, you've spoilt it!"

"Spoilt what?" asked the astonished parents.

"Why," cried the children together, "when you came in the old lady went away!"

"What old lady?"

"The nice lady that sits in the chair by our bedside. She is a dear, we like her. She nods and laughs to us, but when we get out of bed to speak to her she goes away."

"And does she come back?" asked the Rector.

"Yes, Daddy, if we are quiet and stay in bed she comes again."

There is something that impresses about the evidence of children; they have less calculated interests than adults in concocting stories. Who was the old lady, wondered the Rector and his wife, a mother, or some old Nanny haunting the loved scene of her former charges?

Later the Rector, while attending a gathering of clergy, met a friend whom he hadn't seen for years. He was asked where he was living; and, when he mentioned his village and the rectory, the other clergyman said: "What a coincidence! I was Rector there many years ago. In one of the bedrooms there was something queer. My children saw an old lady...."

The second of Mr. Paynter's stories, "The Tregantle Ghost," was partly "proved upon his pulses." He was then interested in the Army Cadet Force and at the time of his curious experience was in camp close to the famous Tregantle Fort, near Plymouth. On the night in question he was put into a huge room, in Tregantle Fort, lit by only one gas jet, bare, with his bed in the corner. When he got into bed he found that the extinguisher for the gas was at the other end of the room. He had to get out of bed to put the light out. "Army beds," said Mr. Paynter, with a wry smile, "are made so that you cannot fall out—indeed you can scarcely move, the blankets are so well tucked in!"

Mr. Paynter spent a dreadful, uncomfortable night in the Fort. "I never got to sleep," he explained, "which is most unusual with me, for I am a good sleeper. I tossed about all night. I had an awful night, full of a nasty feeling of dread and uneasiness. In the morning at breakfast, when one officer asked us how we had slept, I kept quiet."

Then later in the day Mr. Paynter saw the colonel on his way to mess, overtook him, and asked him about the large bare room where he had passed such an unpleasant night.

"Why do you ask?" said the colonel. "Did you sleep well?"

"No," said Mr. Paynter, and told him how very uncomfortable he had been.

"Curious," said the colonel.

"Why, sir?"

"Because that room is supposed to be haunted. We put you in it because we know your reputation as an authority on witchcraft, ghosts, and so on and so forth." Mr. Paynter had had, of course, no idea that the bedroom harboured a sinister reputation.

But the story the Commanding Officer at the Fort told him was sinister enough.

One bitter cold winter night many years ago a party of young officers played cards in a large room in the Fort. One of them, who was losing heavily, resorted to cheating. He was suspected, caught out, and accused. He confessed, and there and then he was tried by his fellow officers.

The court brought in a verdict of "guilty," and he was sentenced to take off all his clothes and spend the rest of the night naked on a terrace. Next morning he was found frozen to death.

Mr. Paynter had tried to sleep in that room where the fatal game of cards had been played, and from which the young man went to his death on the terrace outside. Could the spirit-body of the abused officer have been the cause of Mr. Paynter's restless and unhappy night? In the light of the latest physics, and the reduction of all matter ultimately to electrons and electro-magnetic vibrations, who may confidently assert where the concrete ends and the intangible begins?

As recently as June, 1955, a house, reputed to be haunted, in the Wyndham Square district of Plymouth was blessed by a priest. Though one does not often hear of it, Church blessing and participation, as well as the more solemn service of exorcism, are probably more common than we may imagine. Reasons for believing this haunting to be genuine are, first, the number of people—some seven—who claim to have heard or felt something; secondly, that the house, in a grossly overcrowded area, had known long and very numerous periods without tenants.

The woman, whose household was deeply disturbed, was the wife of a naval rating, with three young children. The family took over two top rooms, converted into a self-contained flat, in October, 1954, and from the start the sailor's wife felt an eerie feeling on entering the inside room, which was intercommunicating. "I felt there was something unseen but very real there." Her husband, as men do, made light of it. When, however, he returned to his ship and his wife was left alone in the house with the children, she gradually became terrified. One day she felt a hand on her shoulder and a tug at her skirt. She asked her husband to try and get compassionate leave, but this was not granted. When he went to sea, a woman friend stayed with her to whom she told nothing of what she had experienced. The friend had a newly born baby, and one night she woke in terror, crying out that someone had placed his hand upon her shoulder and tugged at her nightdress. The sailor's wife was now convinced that her fears were well founded.

Another time, when a married couple were staying in the house, they all heard a voice calling "Betty! Betty!" Nobody had the faintest idea who Betty might be.

So the couple decided to leave the rooms; and the two rooms below having become vacant, the young wife moved into them and closed the door upstairs. But the hand upon her shoulder and the tugging at her dress continued. "Even the cat," she told a reporter, "would burst into the room with its fur bristling, snarling and spitting as if it had been frightened out of its life."

By this time the sailor's wife had had enough; so one stormy night she called on a member of the City Council, who was also a sidesman at St. Michael's Church, Stoke, and who spoke to his vicar, the Rev. Maurice Heath, about the alarming happenings. Mr. Heath got in touch with the Rural Dean, the Rev. J. W. G. Molland. Mr. Molland asked Father N. B. Hansen to investigate.

Father Hansen called at the house, where there were two empty rooms into which nobody went even during daylight hours. After interviewing the sailor's wife, her woman friend and the married couple, he took a serious view and decided to bless the house by means of an ancient ceremony which consists of saying a number of prayers and sprinkling holy water. Though Father Hansen himself experienced no contact with anything supernatural, he thought there might well be something in the story. "These things do happen," he said. "They have happened elsewhere and I see no reason why they should not happen here. These supernatural occurrences are by no means impossible." There has been no fresh apparent manifestation by the "ghost" since the house was blessed by the priest.

But the sailor's wife admitted that even after the blessing she could not sleep for several nights because she was so afraid. She had so many sleepless nights that she consulted a doctor, who prescribed a sedative. She could not sleep without these drugs, and her children were still afraid to walk freely in their own home. There was one rather curious emblem fixed to the door of the upstairs room which the wife and her husband first occupied. It was a medallion, something like an Iron Cross but with rounded edges. In a centre circle appears a Christ-like head and shoulders. Round the circle are the words: Love, Honour, Reparation. Above the head are the letters I.H.S., surmounted by a heart. Asked what he thought of this, Father Hansen replied that he could only guess it to be some symbol of devotion placed there by a previous tenant. He had advised the sailor's wife against having it removed.

Chapter Five

Miscellaneous Poltergeists

THE word "Poltergeist," now anglicised, widely known and accepted by the general public, is a compound of the German verb *polter*, "to make a noise by knocking or tumbling things about, to knock or rattle, to scold or bluster," and the noun *Geist*, a ghost. The easiest definition, then, of a poltergeist would be a noisy, bullying, racketing spirit—if it is a spirit!

For nobody has yet succeeded in explaining the poltergeist. There are different, and conflicting, theories. To hark back to my first chapter, we cannot say simply and exactly what poltergeists are; but we know what they do, we recognise the symptoms of the power that is in them. And the sheer weight of cumulative evidence for their existence is impressive, where the symptoms of poltergeist infestations from the beginning of recorded history, and from all over the globe, remain fairly constant.

In a paper which Mr. Hereward Carrington contributed to the Fifth International Psychical Congress (Oslo, 1935) he said: "Were Poltergeists merely due to trickery, on the one hand, and credulity and superstition, on the other, we should assuredly expect to find them in great numbers in relatively uncivilized countries, or at least in those in which the level of culture is not high.

"But an examination of the material shows that precisely the reverse of this is in fact the case—England, France, Germany, Italy and the United States having the greatest number, while countries such as Haiti, China, Chile, Barbados and Bolivia have the least. ... Certainly, they (the figures) may be explained in part by assuming that—in England, for example—the Press is highly efficient and well organized, and that anything unusual is likely to be reported in the newspapers immediately, while in countries lacking these facilities similar cases are likely to go unrecorded and unreported.

"But this would only bear out my contention that the number of such cases, if known, would be exceedingly large, and would probably run into thousands instead of the hundreds. How account for these thousands of cases? And is it probable that, in all ages of the world and in every country, thousands of spurious phenomena should occur precisely similar in character? That, for example, in Iceland they should be the same as in Sumatra, and a thousand years ago the same as today?"

I have stressed this in quotation because it is both mysterious and cogent when, say, an illiterate native in Papua complains of the same sort of occurrences that have been troubling a black-coated worker's family in a villa in Croydon. Fr. Herbert Thurston, S.J. in his book *Ghosts and Poltergeists* supports the same argument: "The curious fact is that in these and in scores of other cases, some of them centuries old, the same type of phenomena should be recorded by simple and apparently honest people who had no knowledge of psychic literature and who believed their own particular experiences to be unique."

The late Harry Price has neatly said that while a ghost *haunts*, a poltergeist *infests*. Certainly poltergeists seem to like company, while the more normal ghosts generally prefer solitude. And whereas most ghosts seek darkness or the half-light (there are exceptions, the apparently solid, three-dimensional, objective ghost of the Nun at Borley Rectory it is claimed was seen by the four Bull sisters when they were together in sunlight), a poltergeist will cheerfully continue its harmful persecutions undiminished in broad daylight. What then is the range of the paranormal phenomena that poltergeists are capable of producing? The range is maliciously and malevolently wide: first noise, bangings, scratchings, bell-ringings, drummings, "everything from the 'swish' of a silk skirt to an 'explosion' that makes the windows rattle"; then the paranormal movement and displacement of objects, causing their breakage, disappearance and sometimes reappearance. Father Thurston records one amusing example of an unusually friendly attitude on the part of a poltergeist at the home of a Naval Commander Kogelnik in London in 1922, where many things had been broken or disappeared, and the source of energy was thought to be an Austrian maid-servant "Hannie" who was then about sixteen years of age.

"The same afternoon, our teabox lid was missing, and on discovering the loss I said: 'Now wouldn't you be kind enough for once to bring back what you have taken away?' After some minutes the said lid came rolling in from the hall! At this time there were with me in the kitchen both the cook and Hannie, and I had both under observation."

But the entity's usual attitude was decidedly vindictive. Poltergeists are very seldom to be considered as just entertaining, as rather taking ghosts that tease. Commander Kogelnik further reports: "The cook's resentment had been increasing, and towards evening she could no longer refrain from cursing the thing. But the grievous words had hardly escaped her lips when a sharp hissing sound was heard in the air, followed by the frightened cry of the girl, who fled with both hands to her head. Though present, we heard nothing fall, and though we thoroughly inspected the kitchen and the rooms adjoining it, we discovered no object which could have been thrown. It must have been heavy and sharp, for we found her head swelled in one place, and a small cut in another which was bleeding. This was the end of our cook's occult experiences, for she straightway left the house, minus her overcoat, two pairs of stockings and one pair of boots—all discovered some days later in different parts of the house."

That poltergeists, whatever they may be, are capable of understanding and an intelligent contact with certain human beings would seem to be confirmed by an interesting episode told me by my friend, Mrs. Morier, of New House, Penshurst.

"Our resident poltergeist," she said, "is nearly always a quiet and friendly presence and rarely demonstrates unless He or She resents either some person—or unusual household activity—and being either super-sensitive or conceited, there is impatience of non-acceptance when sometimes quite furious action may be taken to insist upon recognition."

"About 1952," she went on, "we had a quite shaking demonstration. A great friend of mine and I were together, she reading *The Times*, myself busy with correspondence, and it was a quiet afternoon in early summer. We were in a small cosy room, no draughts, no wind. There was silence, when my friend suddenly remarked: 'When am I going to see this poltergeist of yours *do* something?' I remember answering: 'Oh, you never will, you don't believe——'

"And then we had it—it was as if a small tornado struck us. Writing materials, books, a heavy ash-tray, papers, were scattered in every direction. The door opened and shut violently, a further door slammed—and there we were in the stillness again surrounded by chaos. 'Your poltergeist I suppose?' remarked my friend, somewhat startled, as she retrieved odds and ends from all over the room. I could only reply: 'Of course; and now look at all this mess to clear up'!"

But poltergeists are not always so harmless. It is wrong, I believe, to regard their antics as merely mischievous in intention. They can be malicious, actively vindictive. Although I have never heard of a poltergeist deliberately murdering a victim, or causing a human being to die of fright, injuries they can and do inflict. For example, Harry Price has told, in his *Poltergeist Over England*, how a Mr. H. F. Russell, a distinguished engineer from Chelmsford, went and paid a visit to Borley Rectory with his two R.A.F. sons, a Wing Commander and a Squadron Leader who were home on leave, on November 12th, 1941. Mr. Russell wrote of his unnatural mishap: "We left the car on the opposite side of the road and my two boys at once entered the house and had a good look round. I followed some twenty yards behind them when I was suddenly seized (so I imagine) and despite my attempts to keep vertical, was dashed to the ground. I felt an unseen, unknown power trying to throw me down, in which it succeeded, and I landed in a pool of mud which necessitated the sending of some clothes to the cleaners." And in *The End Of Borley Rectory*, Price relates how Marianne, the young wife of the Rev. L. A. Foyster who held the benefice at Borley from October 1930 until October 1935, was injured by a poltergeist. "One evening Mrs. Foyster, the Rector's wife, was walking along the passage outside the bathroom, when she was struck a terrific blow under the eye, the resultant cut bleeding copiously. Though she was carrying a candle, she did not see what struck her. Her eye was black for some days. The next night, just as the Foysters had retired to rest, things started flying about the bedroom. A large cotton-reel that had stood on the mantelpiece was projected across the room; it struck the wall and fell on their bed. Then they felt something whizz by their heads and fall with a clatter to the floor. The Rector lit the lamp and explored. The missile was a hammer-head with a portion of the broken handle still *in situ*. The hammer, it was thought, had come from a cupboard where a skull had previously been found!" Doubt has lately been cast on the reliability of Mrs. Foyster's evidence; but she and her husband were just two out of about two hundred witnesses, some of them people of culture and scientific eminence, who vouched for the phenomena at Borley.

That many persons, particularly young girls, have been severely beaten, scratched, slapped, and otherwise tormented and molested by poltergeists, is only too clear from the evidence of the classic cases of The Drummer of Tedworth, The Cock Lane Ghost, the happenings to the Wesleys at Epworth Parsonage, The Great Amherst Mystery in America, to say nothing of the events at Sampford Peverell, near Tiverton in Devon, where the maid-servants were literally beaten black and blue! Perhaps a solution of such a case as the last one, with some explanation of a few well-known "poltergeist girls" such as Esther Cox, Margaret and Katie Fox who gave birth to modern Spiritualism in 1848, Hetty Wesley, Marguerite Rozier, Eleanore Zugun, and Olive W., in Sunderland, must be left to the psycho-analytical approach of the trained scientist of the future.

Possibly the most terrifying example of evil malice on the part of a poltergeist is a very recent one. This was a ghost or elemental, power or entity, which persecuted the Sargent family while they were living in a house at Epsom. My story is based upon the account given by Mrs. Betty Sargent, which appeared in the *Daily Mail* on July 17th, 1950.

One night Mrs. Sargent felt something trying to strangle her. She and her husband left their bedroom, went into the lounge to get away from whatever it might be and tried to sleep on a couch. But in a few minutes the "thing" tried to choke her again.

Another night Mrs. Sargent was lying in bed when a lamp on the small bedside table rose up, came across to her and hit her on the head. Her husband said: "The lamp rose from the table, struck my wife, passed over her bed and landed on mine. I was thoroughly shaken."

Worse was to come, however. "One night," Mr. Sargent said, "Betty was sitting up in bed when something began pulling at her shoulders. It dragged her towards the window, lifting her body so that only her legs and thighs were touching the bed. She cried out for help—I grabbed her by the legs. But whatever it was had very great strength. At first I couldn't hold it, I felt myself being pulled towards the window too. Then all at once it seemed to lose its power and Betty fell."

After that incident Mrs. Sargent, not unnaturally, became really frightened. All the malice, she felt, seemed to be aimed at her, as though the poltergeist was trying to kill her. "If my husband hadn't been there," she pointed out, "I could quite easily have been dragged out of the window, and it would have been written off as suicide."

Then came an anti-climax, the nylon incident. The ghost used often to be active during the day; it would disarrange bed-clothes, upset cosmetics, throw pyjamas on to the floor. Then one day it removed a pair of nylons from their cellophane packet, tore them, and dropped them on the floor. Mrs. Sargent found them hopelessly laddered, ruined. "If ghosts have sex," was her comment, "it makes me think it must be a woman. It was such a catty sort of thing to do!"

Poltergeists are known to have some mysteriously close connexion with fire and water. They are often incendiaries, fire-raisers; and, apparently, through the agency of these too commonly supposed harmless ghosts, scores of people have been badly burnt. Lighted matches have fallen from ceilings; mattresses have unaccountably started to smoke and smoulder; and in 1929 at a house in Lillington Avenue, Leamington, during other poltergeist disturbances, "a saucepan of *cold* water, containing peeled potatoes, began to boil over at midnight," when there was no fire in the kitchen range on which the saucepan rested. If the poltergeist is not a discarnate entity, "the ghost that once was man," as Tennyson put it, but rather an elemental or some kind of Nature-spirit corresponding to the lower elemental nature of man, we might expect this link with the four elements, earth, air, fire and water. It must be significant, surely, as Harry Price has pointed out, "that both the two famous 'poltergeist rectories' in this country should have been destroyed by fire: Epworth in February, 1709, and Borley in February, 1939." The Ghost House at Sampford Peverell also was burnt down and entirely lost some ten years ago.

However, it is not necessarily the most sensational cases that carry the greatest conviction. Mr. Hugh Dent, who is a schoolmaster at Plymouth College, has kindly sent me the following factual account, with his disarming comment: "Here's our little 'wasserpolter' as promised. It reads as dull as dishwater, I've deliberately underwritten it because I hate glamorized ghosts." But I do not agree that it is dull.

"The house was built in the new fashionable northern suburb of Plymouth in about 1850, solid, of stone. In 1935 the landlord put a door at the top of the stairs to make the upper storey into a self-contained flat, which was leased by a newly married couple at Christmas, 1936. The bedroom, with twin single beds two feet apart, had no flaw in the ceiling, no handbasin, no taps, and the chimney was completely blocked by a built-in gas fire. The first Easter brought the first visitor, Mr. Hugh Dent's sister, a young schoolmistress. Just before she arrived Mrs. Lorna Dent went into the bedroom and turned the eiderdowns satin-side up, for show. Miss Dent, of Prestbury, Macclesfield, arrived, was shown the new flat, admired the eiderdowns, and preceded her hostess to the sitting-room, Mrs. Dent shutting the bedroom door after them. A few minutes later Mrs. Dent went back into the bedroom, to find, standing on the eiderdown of her own bed, a quantity of water; how much is difficult to estimate, but enough—when all three had admired the phenomenon—to make it necessary to carry the eiderdown by its corners and empty the water into the bath. The three went back to the bedroom, and after some fantastic guessing Miss Dent suggested: "Let's agree to stay here until we have found the solution." Had they stuck to her proposal they would still be there!

"Months passed and the nine days' wonder had been almost forgotten. The couple were reading in bed and Mrs. Dent put her book down on the eiderdown while she reached across for something. As she picked the book up again she found it slimy, and the red dye from off the wet back marked her hands. There was no normal water within reach. On a third occasion Mr. Dent, from the other bed, was about to stretch to put out the reading-lamp on the table between the beds when the sound of splashing exactly where he was caused him to duck his head. But no water was either seen or felt that time. It must have been eighteen months after the first water showed itself that Dr. Sybil Hawkes, of Mannamead, Plymouth, a woman doctor with a large practice, examined Mrs. Dent on her bed. After the examination Mrs. Dent went out of the room, and when she came back Dr. Hawkes said: 'I'm sorry. I seem to have spilt some water on the eiderdown but I haven't had any water, and there isn't any in the room.' There certainly was water, though, near the head of the eiderdown! The doctor made the comment: 'When you've had as much experience of life and death as I have, you'll know that there are a lot of things we can't explain.'

"It was agreed by almost everybody that the flat had a perfectly 'comfortable atmosphere'; neither Mr. nor Mrs. Dent felt any sense of trouble, but again and again they were conscious of a ghostly visitor coming to the sitting-room across the landing. When Mr. Dent was out lecturing in the evenings, his wife often noticed that the dog was conscious of someone; this the husband dismissed to himself for some months as probably imaginary. One evening, however, the Dents were both in, when their dog gave the normal growl that she always gave if someone rang the street door bell a storey below. The couple felt, rather than heard, somebody coming up the stairs: then the dog went to the door, sniffed the unseen visitor at the door; and, behaving as though she recognised 'him,' followed him over to the chair where Mr. Dent was sitting. Hugh Dent got out of his chair pretty quickly. The dog sniffed up the legs that weren't there, and then settled down satisfied that it was friendly. On several occasions both Mr. and Mrs. Dent had the same sensations of the visitor coming up the stairs, and more than once they called out or went across to the door.

"In 1940 the Dents left the flat when Hugh Dent was called up. But it was not long before heavy air-raids had made so many Plymouth roofs no longer waterproof that inquiries about the persistence of the phenomenon of unexplained water would have been pointless. Moreover, since the flat changed hands the Dents did not wish to worry the new tenants with any suggestion which might have made them less comfortable in a flat that had only this minor, if macabre, snag."

Surely Psychical Research, very much "in the air" today, is among the most exciting researches of our century? As I write a week's conference of twenty-nine European and American professors has just ended at Newnham College, Cambridge, organized, as *The Times* for July 18th, 1955 reports, by the S.P.R. Among the phenomena considered were hauntings, poltergeist phenomena, telepathic dreams, apparitions and similar happenings in various parts of the world. The professors resolved that "discovery, careful sifting, authentication and intense study of a large number of cases, including recent cases, should be undertaken on a world-wide scale." One distinguished delegate to this Cambridge conference, Dr. Hornell Hart, Professor of Sociology at Duke University, North Carolina, in a concluding article in a series on "Apparitions and Ghostly Visitations," which appeared in *The Star* on July 18th—after pointing out that "past leaders in psychical research have been men and women trained in other lines of intellectual activity" (Sir William Crookes and Sir William Barrett were physicists, Dr. J. B. Rhine was a biologist) —draws attention to "the most promising pioneering now being done in psychical research, the work of a distinguished geologist."

"His name," writes Professor Hornell Hart, "is Dr. R. Crookall, Ph.D., of Langley Road, Chippenham, Wiltshire. He has written massive treatises on paleontology and regional geology. His articles are scattered thickly through learned periodicals.

"But the major work on which he is investing the ripe years of his scientific maturity consists in the classification and analysis of cases bearing upon the essential nature of human personality and of its survival of bodily death.

"If Dr. Crookall's preliminary findings are supported by further research these conclusions will (in my opinion) provide the greatest forward surge towards illuminating man's destiny in eternity which has been achieved since Myers published his basic study." Can anything be of greater personal importance, or of more absorbing general interest, to mankind than this?

In the pages of the National Press are to be found, apparently from quite honest, ordinary, matter-of-fact people, numerous complaints of many uncanny happenings. Of course to carry complete conviction, each one of these cases would need the most careful and patient investigation, with knowledge of the psychology and the past and present circumstances of the human beings involved. Nevertheless, here are three such cases which have been reported in the Press within the last two summer months.

The first is taken from the *Evening Standard*. Mr. Francis Cole, groundsman at the Mid-Kent Golf Club, Gravesend, declares that he has been driven out of his home at the Overcliffe, Gravesend, by a poltergeist. There were tappings on his bedroom window, he heard shuffling footsteps. He was unable to sleep at night; doors opened of their own accord; he saw as he sat up, sleepless, in bed, his black cat spitting with fear and fury as the doors of a built-in cupboard began to open and close. The house is reputed to have been the scene of a murder during the nineteenth century.

The second case is that of a young Llanelly couple who have had to leave their home because of a ghost. My account is based upon cuttings from their issues of June 14th and 15th, 1955, sent me by *The Western Mail and South Wales News*, Cardiff.

Mr. Jack Rees, aged twenty-nine, is a steel erector employed at Carmarthen Bay Power Station. He, with his wife of twenty-three and son of seven, lived at a house in Bryn Terrace, Llanelly, until driven away by an apparition which appeared at their bedside at midnight on Thursday, June 2nd. They have returned to their old home only once—and then spent a sleepless night.

During the three years they lived in the house, before the climax, other strange things had happened; as one of them put it to a *Western Mail* reporter: "knockings at the door with no one there and smashed crockery galore." Their spaniel bitch, Nell, had growled at night and taken a strong dislike to the house.

At midnight on June 2nd Mr. Rees was awakened by the sound of dripping water, and, looking up, saw the apparition some three feet from the bed. It had exceptionally broad shoulders. "I stared at it and studied it for some three minutes," Mr. Rees said. "It did not move. I jerked my head suddenly and it backed away. My wife woke up, took one look at it and screamed. It then disappeared."

Mrs. Rees said she first saw the ghost on the upstairs landing when she and her husband returned from stock car racing at Neath. "I screamed and ran away, but later thought I had been seeing things and put it out of my mind." Now Mr. and Mrs. Rees are attending spiritualist meetings together to try to solve the problem. There is a theory that the malevolent spirit is that of an old retired sea captain, who had been a miser when he lived in the house about seventy years ago. It is said that he had exceptionally broad shoulders.

My last newspaper-reported case is from Birmingham, and appeared, prominent as an illustrated article by Mr. Derek Agnew, in *The People* on Sunday, July 17th, 1955. Although the details in many hauntings would seem bound to repeat themselves, there is one feature about the plight of Mr. and Mrs. Pell that makes their case stand out. Apart from the cheap rent, the Pells had every reason to continue living at 32, Coxwell Road, Ladywell, Birmingham, if they possibly could. After living with his wife and five children in a condemned house for two years, Frank Pell, aged thirty-one and an ex-paratrooper with a brave war record, had at last reached the top of the housing list of 50,000 people waiting for a house. Mrs. Pell was overjoyed when she saw the pleasant, though older type, three-bedroom council house in a quiet road, and the family moved in at the end of May. "It had been newly decorated, was as clean as a new pin, and seemed the answer to our prayers," she said. "We sent for Father Francis Etherington to bless it for us. He is our local Catholic priest." From their photographs in the paper the Pells look like perfectly normal, nice, working-class people, with no nonsense about them. Yet very soon they were living with relatives in wretched surroundings a few streets away, and today nothing would induce either of them to return to No. 32, a house which Frank Pell swears is haunted. He knows now that the previous tenants also left hurriedly.

What was it that drove the Pells to leave? The week-end of its arrival, the family was woken by unexplained banging doors. Loud thuds came from the ceiling above the kitchen. Frank Pell noticed strange smells, "like garlic, turning to a smell of burning rubber." However, they dismissed all this as "odd" and carried on.

Then in June came tragedy. They awoke one morning to find their month-old baby dead in bed beside them. No mark was on her, but at the inquest Professor Webster said the infant was in perfect health but had died from accidental suffocation. "Yet it was a hot night," sobbed Mrs. Pell, "and we had thrown back

"He lived at a house in Bryn-terrace, Llanelly, until driven away by an apparition which appeared at their bedside at midnight on Thursday, June 2nd."

the bed-clothes. If I rolled on her during my sleep, there would surely have been bruises on so small a child." The Pells buried their daughter, and tried again to be happy in their new home.

But the ghost—or poltergeist—refused them any peace. Each night, generally beginning at 10.20 p.m., taps persisted in coming from the ceiling above the kitchen, which were heard by relatives and friends as well as by Mr. and Mrs. Pell. The banging of doors continued, at intervals, during the small hours of the morning; the temperature of the bedroom above the kitchen changed almost hourly; and the strange smells were present in different parts of the house.

A few days after the baby's death, Alan, aged four, said one evening: "Did baby go with the little white dog?"

Frank and his wife grew pale. "What dog, Alan?"

"The little white dog who comes and sits on my bed sometimes. I saw him sitting on baby's face the night baby left us." Mrs. Pell broke down.

Frank Pell, with the police, searched the house, but they found nothing. Father Etherington came with a rosary and Holy Water to exorcise the house. As he stood with a relative in the upstairs room, he heard the tappings, also mysterious whisperings, described as "like someone talking close to a microphone." Later he said to the worried Frank Pell: "I have done all that is possible. For your health and the health of your family you should leave the house. It is bad for you." But Frank Pell looked grim, and said he would fight back.

One day Frank was shaving downstairs when he heard the whispering again, just behind him. "I knew that only my wife was in the house," he tried to explain. "I rushed to the stairs to see if it was her. She was standing at the top of the stairs, mouth open as if screaming, but I could hear no sound. I started to clamber up the stairs. Then I stopped dead. There was a kind of invisible barrier I couldn't break. I caught hold of the banisters and heaved. Suddenly I broke through. At once I could hear my wife's sobs and screams. She said the voices had been whispering to her as well."

So the Pell family left Coxwell Road precipitously—without

even packing a bag or making a bed! Frank Pell's niece, June Hadley aged twenty-two, with her fiancé, Dennis Savage aged twenty-five, went to the house to collect the Pells's belongings; but they, too, said "never again"; for they had heard the strange tappings for themselves.

Mr. Agnew and a *People* photographer stayed all night in the house, and did confirm changes of temperature and also a musty smell that came and went in certain rooms. They saw nothing; but discovered a faint gas leak in one room, which might have accounted for the smell of rubber. A full check on the house is to be made by surveyors at the demand of Birmingham Council. Meanwhile, Mr. and Mrs. Pell are to be rehoused, with their four remaining children. But, whatever the result of the council's investigation, they remain convinced that the house is haunted.

My next tale of a comparatively mild example of poltergeist infestation I can vouch for, since the people concerned are personal friends of mine of more than a quarter of a century's standing. Only the name of the house shall be fictitious. It is the story of an unlucky house, not an old house, but a fairly modern one, semi-detached, built probably about 1902, and overlooking the famous Prestbury golf course in Cheshire.

In the early nineteen twenties Harold and Sally Collier, a young married couple whose livelihood depended upon the cotton industry, were living in Prestbury and had heard something of the bad reputation this house had acquired in the neighbourhood. There was a history of ill-luck: a young man had died in it of tuberculosis; the next owners had always been ailing, and when the wife had a baby she nearly lost her life, although there had been no reason to expect a difficult birth. There was talk in Prestbury about Bucklands, which was said to be an unhappy, evil-fated house.

One day Sally Collier lay indisposed in bed, when her father came into the bedroom. Her father had bought a plot of land, on which he was intending to build a house for the young couple. Now he told Sally that he had a surprise for her—he had sold the plot of land, and had just bought them a house instead, which had a nice garden overlooking the golf course! Sally went cold to her bones. She knew intuitively that the house her father had bought was Bucklands, and she could have loudly screamed that she did not want it. But she hadn't the heart to offend her father by doing this. So the Colliers moved into Bucklands in the spring of 1925.

At this time the Colliers had a baby girl, Joy, of three years old. Almost at once Sally had her second child, Anne. These babies demanded nursemaids; and in the following few years there were three Nannies, for they left in quick succession. The first Nanny was Ellen Bull, a girl of seventeen and of somewhat sub-normal intelligence, slow and very simple, who died at the age of nineteen of an obscure, perhaps mental, disease. Both she and the maid complained of hearing sinister steps going up and down the stairs. She was replaced by Megan Davies, a Welsh Norland Nurse, aged twenty-four, who left all in a moment and flatly refused to give the reason why. The third nurse, Nanny Jones, was a red-haired harum-scarum girl who went on holiday and was killed in a motor-cycle smash. A woman, who came in daily to do the housework, one morning ran straight out of the house, as white as a shroud, after saying that she had heard somebody tell her to give a message to the people next door. She had thought it was Sally, but had looked and there was no one there. She never came back.

One Sunday during lunch Sally and Harold Collier both heard a curious tinkling, falling noise coming from the oak corner-cupboard, where their best glass was kept. Sally opened the door of the cupboard, when a shower of pieces of broken glass fell down over the shelves. Most of the glass was valuable wedding-present glass, some of it Waterford glass. Sally still keeps a large plate, with a big round hole right through the thickest part.

Such supernormal occurrences were separated by months, but they always seemed to happen on Sundays when Harold was at home. Once there was a colossal bang during the mid-day meal, as Harold had risen to fetch a dish of fruit from the dresser. He found the dresser—like the Lady of Shalott's mirror—cracked from side to side. Today it has a half-inch crack clean through the wood!

Yet once again in the middle of a Sunday lunch both Sally and Harold heard a tremendous smashing sound in the pantry. Sally rushed into the kitchen, found the servant and the nursemaid, and demanded which of them had been smashing things—or could it be the kitten? The girls could only shake their heads. They had heard the noise too, in the pantry. On investigation it was found that havoc had overtaken the best Minton dessert service: three dessert dishes had large triangular pieces blown, apparently, forcibly out of them! Pieces of precious china were scattered all over the floor.

Before leaving for a holiday in the summer of 1928, Harold Collier had seen that the stop-cock was turned off; he had himself attended to this, so that he knew that the water-supply to the house was turned off at the main. While they were away, neighbours communicated with the Colliers to inform them that their house, judging by the quantity of water pouring from it, must be flooded! Arriving home, Harold and Sally found that the water was about three or four inches deep in the rooms on the ground floor and that the carpets were floating. The wet and dampness had done much damage to furniture, including an antique grandfather clock.

Today the S.P.R. is interested in extra-sensory perception and in genuine cases of precognition, unaccountable foreknowledge of the future. During the last years of the 'twenties Sally Collier's father, who was dying, foresaw that financial disaster would overtake her husband and had asked Sally's eldest brother to look after the couple. Owing to the great depression and consequent crisis in the cotton industry, the disaster happened. Shortly after the old man's death, because of the delay due to the necessity of probate of Sally's father's will, the Colliers had hardly a £5 note left. They sold the unhappy, unlucky house Bucklands.

In 1929 a family from the Canadian Rockies rented Bucklands for a year. Before they moved in some of their huge packing-cases had been delivered to the house and firmly stored. The house was locked. But people had heard a terrific crash. It was discovered that a packing-case had turned over on its side and much that was in it was broken. The wife from Canada had twins in this house, with forty-eight hours' labour between each delivery, and she finally went raving mad.

A picturesque, well-accredited story of unexplained, alarming forces at work comes from the beautiful small Sussex village of Burwash. If you look down from the high Burwash ridge on a late and fading summer evening, northwards over the valley, you may see a grey manor house about a mile away; it is a house with a tall tower and square windows, creeper-covered, and set in dark trees; often at this time of the year scarves of white mist loiter, clinging about the house, lending it the perfect appearance and atmosphere for a haunting.

Some thirty years ago, about 1925, this house stood empty, but a Lady B—— intended shortly to move in. However, she couldn't do so before the house had been thoroughly rid of many thousands of unwelcome tenants. Swarms of bees had forced a vacant possession, building honeycombs in most of the chimneys, entirely blocking them up. In the tower there were squares of solid honey as big as a door.

Nothing could be done, of course, until the bees had come in and settled for the night. So one evening in mid-summer Mr. "Laddie" Richardson, who was then aged twenty and sexton at Burwash church, with his friend Mr. Frank Killick who was a little older, walked down across the fields to the manor house in order to drive the bees out of the chimneys. The two friends worked together in the house from 10 p.m. until 1 a.m., beginning by lighting sulphur fires in the lounge and dining-room grates to induce the bees to fly up and out from under the sacking placed over the chimney-tops. Every half hour or so they took it in turns to visit the roof, where there was a yard-wide parapet, to see if the bees were leaving as they hoped. They used a fourteen-foot batten to push down the chimneys to help clear the solid matter. Both men, unknown to the other, have given me their separate accounts of the uncanny things that happened that night. Their two accounts tally.

"Laddie" Richardson (who has broadcast and made gramophone recordings of such old Sussex songs as "Buttercup Joe" and "The Sow") told me that for a long time he tried to hide his misgivings from Killick. He felt, as he went out of the room and started to climb the stairs, that he was not alone; he heard footsteps; doors opened and shut again after him, like a sinister echo. And it was the same with Frank Killick, but he said nothing. Killick said he remembers Laddie coming down "looking sort of agitated and windy." Presently it came to the point of arguments as to who should go up on to the roof the next time—"You go," "No, you go," "No, it's your turn this time," until they were obliged to confess their fears to each other. Then they both went up together; but the weird feeling and the noises happened once more just the same, the footsteps, the sense of someone or something following them, and the doors opening and shutting like an echo.

By 1 a.m. they had both had enough and decided to quit. They were tired and dirty and thoroughly afraid. They went downstairs through a basement, to wash in an open-air water-tank in the yard. They carried a hurricane lamp and, as they were going past the kitchen, they both heard the loud sounds of somebody washing-up, the clink of crockery, plates rattling as they were put into the rack. But the kitchen was empty. And then, in the yard by the water-tank, the worst thing happened. They had started to wash their hands when something huge and floppy and white came slowly flapping at them and hit the stable wall with a thick muffled thud and seemed to fall down right in front of them. They bent to look for, perhaps, the body of an owl—but there was nothing there! They both admit to having been terrified, and made an extra two-mile circuit along the road, rather than return home through the fields.

Two days after Lady B—— had moved into the house, her maids reported that they had heard someone walking about in the house. Mysterious door-shuttings were heard also by Lady B—— and she informed the police, who asked if Killick had been there. He had not, and the solution to the trouble was never found. Within a week the manor house appeared to be normal, and I have heard of no haunting since that one summer.

Chapter Six

Brede Place, Rye, and Reysons Farm

BREDE PLACE, seven miles from unique Rye, is itself perfect and unique; standing on a little plateau beyond a big park, it overlooks a lush and radiant valley where formerly swept an arm of the salt sea. Undoubtedly, as Sir Edwin Lutyens has said, Brede Place is the most interesting and haunted inhabited house in Sussex. It is also a lyric in stone and brick; to be more precise it is built out of blocks of the sarsen stone, sandstone, of the county, and with small pink bricks of later Tudor origin, which together proclaim its over six centuries of existence. The public may see and enjoy Brede Place on every Wednesday afternoon of the year.

This house was first called Ford Place, after the ford which made possible the crossing of the stretch of sea that came in from between Rye and what is today Winchelsea. Although the original portion of the present beautiful old mansion was built by Sir Thomas atte Forde towards the middle of the fourteenth century, it was the Oxenbridge family (one of whom is said to have purchased Brede Place from a Joan atte Forde) who, in the sixteenth century, carried out the Tudor alterations and embellishments. The most noted Oxenbridge was Sir Goddard who, besides much else, "placed oak panelling in several of the principal rooms and built fireplaces and doorways in Caen stone decorated with carved Tudor emblems"; but of the "giant" Oxenbridge wild tales were told, notably that he ate the flesh of babies until the villagers, enraged by his excesses, sawed him in half at Groaning Bridge with a wooden saw! Sir Goddard Oxenbridge is one of the ghosts said to haunt Brede Place; although smugglers of subsequent centuries may have had an interest in keeping this fearsome legend alive. "Such nonsensical stories are still mentioned in the village to this day," remarks Mrs. Clare Sheridan, the sculptor cousin of Sir Winston Churchill, in her lovely book *My Crowded Sanctuary*. However, she goes on to admit her belief that "because there is never smoke without a little fire, that some member of the Oxenbridge family behaved unseemly." There exists a likely tale of a feud between an Oxenbridge and his neighbour Cheney, a quarrel about the boundary of properties which adjoined, when to make an end of the matter Cheney slyly entered Oxenbridge's house and murdered him in his sleep! The author, Mr. Thurston Hopkins, has carried the yarn farther, telling how the corpse was hidden by Cheney and his men in the belfry of a church tower, where it lay undiscovered for five years until a maidservant at Brede, who had loved the dead man, traced the crime and informed the Oxenbridges. So one night the family descended upon Cheney's house, set fire to it, seized Cheney, took him and tied him to the clapper of the church bell and rung him to death! Mrs. Sheridan comments on this: "A pretty story, and gives a likely picture of the times, though there seems to be no proof of its reliability."

Nevertheless, Mrs. Clare Sheridan has no doubt whatever that Brede Place is haunted. Her only son, Richard Brinsley Sheridan, inherited the mansion on his twenty-first birthday, in September, 1936. His tragic death came four months later, following an operation for appendicitis in Algeria, when the historic property passed to his mother and she was the owner during the war. Of the ghosts she writes about so movingly in her sensitive, most interesting book; of Martha; of the tree spirits; and of Father John (the house is said to have been built upon the site of a religious shrine) I will say nothing; for they are alive in her pages which must remain her sanctuary.

Before she married Mrs. Sheridan was a Frewen, and this family, whose main estates were at Brickwall, Northiam, and in Ireland, has owned Brede Place since Sir Edward Frewen bought it in 1708, excepting the years 1947 to 1950 when it belonged to a Captain Traquair who, fortunately, had taste and put in fitted carpets, modern bathrooms and a good deal of suitable furniture. But when Captain Traquair was killed in a motor-car accident in 1950, it was found that he had had no money and the estate was declared bankrupt. Romantically it was bought back into the Frewen family by the present owner, Mr. Roger Frewen, who is Clare Sheridan's nephew, in 1952, the year he married. Mr. Frewen and his wife are bringing up a baby son and daughter in a house that is a treasury of history and beauty and which they both love.

When I was most kindly entertained there by Mr. Frewen, he gave me not only some news of the ghosts, but told me that he felt his presence in Brede Place was certainly approved of, perhaps blessed, by the spirits of his ancestors. He felt this especially about his grandmother, Mrs. Moreton Frewen (one of the Miss Jeromes of New York before she married, and the sister of Lady Randolph Churchill) who restored and beautified the house, taking also a great interest in designing and laying out the grounds and rose-gardens between 1900 and her death in June, 1935, at the age of eighty-three. About Christmas 1954 at Brede Place a psychic manifestation of benevolence was conveyed by a pleasant odour. Roger Frewen was sleeping in the main bedroom when, during one evening, he went into a small adjoining room, now a bathroom, which in days gone by had always served as a sort of lumber-room for all the personal belongings of his grandmother. As soon as he opened the door, he experienced a strong wave of violet perfume, unforgettably the scent Mrs. Moreton Frewen used, the sensory impact of which brought back to him the room as it had been in his grandmother's time. He told me that he had the moving feeling of confidence that this was the old lady's characteristic way of conveying her delight at what he was doing for Brede Place.

During the year 1898 Mrs. Moreton Frewen lent Brede Place to Stephen Crane, the brilliant American novelist, who, until his untimely death in 1900, made what was then the rather dilapidated old mansion, with its uncanny sights and sounds, his home, where he entertained many literary friends. Mrs. Edith R. Jones, today the wife of a Massachusetts architect, in the summer of 1899 when she was a young girl living in England, was absorbed into the exciting household of Stephen Crane, and his magnetic wife Cora, at Brede. After nearly four decades she contributed an article to *The Atlantic Monthly* about that enchanted time so vivid that remembrance of things past sounds like yesterday.

In *Stephen Crane at Brede* Edith Jones writes: "The Cranes always said that the 'modern improvements' were made in Elizabethan days. There was no running water—it had to be pumped outdoors and brought in. No gas or electric lights, just lamps and candles. Huge open fireplaces. Many rooms in the house were left unfurnished. Cora had found a lot of lovely old four-poster beds being used as chicken coops in neighbouring farmyards and had bought them for a song and had them rubbed down and fitted with mattresses.... The beautiful big oak-panelled hall, where we lived most of the time, was full of comfortable couches and chairs and pretty tables with lamps and plants and books. The dining-room had a long refectory table and rushes on the floor from the meadows by the brook. There was a chapel in the house, but it had long been used as a storeroom. The Cranes stored apples there." Today the chapel is beautifully restored, spick and span, and contains Clare Sheridan's bleached pine statue of an expectant Madonna, which she calls "Ave Maria."

"The house was supposed to be haunted and no one from

Brede village would work there after dark. I slept in the haunted room, and Stephen insisted that a dog or two should sleep there too. He was afraid someone might try to play practical jokes and scare me. Outside my windows was thick ivy in which white owls roosted, and their "hoo-hoo-hoos" were eerie if you didn't know where they came from. The room had three doors, leading to other rooms or halls. When I went up to dress for dinner, I would carefully close each door. A moment later look fearsomely over my left shoulder. Door number one would be open. Then, over my right shoulder, door number two open, and a little further to the right, door number three. I always turned slowly and always had the same spooky feeling. But the doors, I knew, were not really bewitched. They all had old slippery wooden latches which had to be pegged to stay shut.

"When I was lying in bed at night, I seemed to hear babies crying, or a coach-and-four would come trundling from a distance, the horses' hoof-beats pounding louder and louder over my head. I loved it, because it was the wind making the rafters creak and groan. . . .

"Joseph Conrad came often to Brede, but his wife was not well at that time and I never met her. . . . I liked Mr. Conrad the most of any of the Brede guests. He was charming, quiet and courteous. I was shy and inclined to listen rather than to talk. He would discuss books with me as seriously as with his fellow writers.

"I wish I knew how to describe the atmosphere of Brede. I have never known two people more deeply in love with one another than were Stephen and Cora. Their sweetness and consideration each for the other were touching and charming. Each was extremely sensitive, each protective. Cora ran the household for Stephen's comfort and happiness. She followed his every change of mood. If he wanted silence, he had silence. If he wanted company and gaiety, he had them. They were fine people, both of them. They were *good*. Always they were good. Not only were they 'good' to me. They were ethically good. They were kind. They were just.

"Stephen had candid grey eyes and tawny hair and mustache, both rather shaggy. He was slender but not delicate-looking. Cora was short. She had great dignity and quiet charm. Her hair was pure gold, her skin exquisite. She was a woman of great distinction. . . .

"When Mr. Conrad, the H. G. Wellses, A. E. W. Mason, Mr. Pugh, and others were at Brede, we would sit around the huge fireplace in the hall in the evenings and everyone would have to tell stories. I remember one told by Mr. Mason. When he was a lad he went to stay with a classmate whom he had visited before. They arrived late at night when everyone had gone to bed. The young host showed Mason to the room he had had on other visits, and Mason went to bed and to sleep. He wakened to hear groans and to see a white figure floating between ceiling and floor. Terrified, he pulled the bedclothes over his head and finally went to sleep. In the morning he found that a poor young maid had hanged herself from the tester of his big four-poster bed. She had thought the room was empty."

With Christmas 1899 in the offing, Stephen Crane conceived the notion that a play, "The Ghost," should be written by a whole bevy of distinguished authors! As I write I have before me a copy of a pamphlet about this by John D. Gordon (The New York Public Library, 1953), which reproduces as a frontispiece a photograph of "a unique copy of Stephen Crane theatrical program, in the Berg Collection." The title runs: *The Ghost*. Written by Mr. Henry James, Mr. Robert Barr, Mr. George Gissing, Mr. Rider Haggard, Mr. Joseph Conrad, Mr. H. B. Marriott-Watson, Mr. H. G. Wells, Mr. Edwin Pugh, Mr. A. E. W. Mason and Mr. Stephen Crane. *Brede School House*, December 28th, 1899. 7.45 P.M. Needless to say the play was "utter nonsense," a scene, a sentence, even a word only being required from each author—"It," "they," "you" would do—and "Mr. Mason as the Ghost had the only real role." The production seems to have been a kind of revue, with dancing and singing; for example, the third act opened with a chorus, "Oh, ghost, we're waiting for you to come," sung on a darkened stage, and tastefully accompanied on the piano by Mrs. H. G. Wells. The pamphlet concludes by assuring us that in the lost manuscript of *The Ghost*, we have "lost nothing more than a curiosity. Yet any curiosity that involved such an array of talent is a ghost that can never quite be laid."

There is a sequel to Mrs. Edith Jones's article, long after the deaths of Stephen and Cora Crane. "Almost thirty years later, when my daughter Katherine was fourteen, I took her to England and to Brede.... Into the big hall we went. It looked very different from the Cranes's time. Beautiful furniture, fine pictures. Soon, in came Mrs. Frewen, a little old lady, very changed from earlier days. She hugged us both and told Katherine about the happy times we had had together. She showed us all over the house. Her bedroom was a room that had been empty in our time. In it was a bed that had belonged to Queen Anne. The chapel had been re-dedicated, and over the altar was a copy of the Descent from the Cross which her daughter, Clare Sheridan, had sculptured for the Kitchener Memorial. House and Garden were full of beauty.

"I told Mrs. Frewen that I had slept in the haunted room for five months. She said that when they first moved back to Brede, after their house in Ireland had been burned during the Troubles, she had invited her sister, Lady Randolph Churchill, to pay her a visit. She put her in the haunted room. Next morning, Lady Randolph left in a hurry and said she never would enter Brede Place again. But Winston came and slept there and didn't mind."

Mr. Roger Frewen has lent me a most interesting, hitherto unpublished, letter concerning the ghostly occupants of Brede Place during the early years of this century, with his permission to reproduce it. The letter is from A. P. Sinnett, who was a Vice-President of the Theosophical Society and written to Mrs. Moreton Frewen. Mrs. Sheridan has told how, when Mr. Sinnett stayed with them many years ago, he said: "I am not surprised you feel the house is haunted—I can tell you something——" But her father stopped him, because he was afraid to hear. A. P. Sinnett had visited Brede Place, with an occult friend, in 1910 to make some investigations, and later wrote this letter to Mrs. Frewen:

> 59, Jermyn Street, S.W.
> July 21, 1912.
>
> Dear Mrs. Frewen,
>   I have heard a good deal since I was with you, about the astral frequenters of Brede Place. The room I slept in is frequented by a lady who died there suddenly under tragic circumstances about 150 years ago. She is in no way hostile to you or anybody, but she sometimes tries to manifest herself and does occasionally give rise to noises in the effort to materialise. She did want to get in touch with me when I was there but one of my occult friends who came along to look after me would not allow her to do so, as it would (so I am told) have drawn too much vitality from me. I am rather sorry she was not allowed to have her own way as it would have been very interesting.
>   There is also an old man who frequents the place. He lived there some hundreds of years ago and is fond of the house. He, it appears, took notice of me from my first arrival, recognising me as connected with the occult world in which he was deeply interested in life, and I am told that when I was out of the body in sleep I had a long talk with him.
>   He is altogether friendly to you and the family and endeavours to be helpful to you, by carrying to your sons the thought forms which your love for them engenders. This may not be very intelligible to you, but some day when you are up in London I might be able to see you and talk it all over.
>
> Ever yours sincerely,
> A. P. Sinnett.

Soon after Richard Brinsley Sheridan acquired Brede Place he let it, and before the war his female tenant spoke of seeing the ghost of a lady. But, apparently, this haunting has been recorded right up to Coronation Year. Mr. Roger Frewen tells me that from May 1st to 3rd, 1953, during the Easter holidays, a friend of his and her schoolboy son, aged fifteen, from Harrow, stayed with him. The boy slept in the room that Stephen Crane had once used as a study. The boy woke up at 2 a.m. to see, standing in the bedroom a lady with very high shoulders and wearing a

Brede Place, Sussex.

large floating dress. His first reaction was that it was his mother who had come in from the bedroom next door; but when he saw that she was nobody living, though she looked fairly solid, he was terrified and hid himself under the bedclothes, where they found him in the morning still curled up and buried.

Rye, a picturesque town with so venerable an atmosphere, might be expected to be the source and scene of numerous ghost stories, and this is so. I have space to narrate only two, but they offer a contrast. They were brought to my notice by a well-known antiquary and scholar who lives in Rye, yet who wishes to remain anonymous since they were not his "personal adventures in the Spirit World." He believes them, nevertheless, to be true records of stories told to him in all sincerity in the year 1935 when he was collecting genuine ghost stories. The first I will give more or less in the words of a simple soul who once was a cook in a house in Watchbell Street.

"Once I was sitting," this lady said, "on a seat on the Lookout (a vantage point that overlooks the Marshes) when I noticed, sitting by my side, an old monk in a brown gown. I did not like it, so I went indoors to my kitchen. But there was the monk! So I said to him, 'You ought not to be here, my Lady would not like it.' He replied, 'But I live here.' I said, 'You don't!'; but he replied, 'I do live here—I'm buried in the garden.' This upset me but I was not afraid. He continued, 'Years ago I was sent down here from Canterbury to look after the young monks at this church in Rye, because they had got out of hand. They did not wash before Mass, and were behaving scandalously. So I reprimanded them, and tried to bring them to order. They would not listen, they rebelled and killed me. Then they buried me in your garden. I want you to get me buried in consecrated ground. I plead with you to do this!' Then he vanished. Being much concerned, I told my Mistress all about it. She consulted Father Benaventure, the priest in charge of St. Anthony's church here, who very wisely said, 'You cannot dig up all the garden to find the bones. I will come and consecrate the garden.' This the priest did, and from that day there was peace in our house."

The second story, "Footsteps in the Night," is more attractively romantic. During the long winter evenings of the year 1934 a middle-aged woman, who was the owner of a house at the corner of Watchbell Street, sometimes heard light pattering footsteps coming along the street when all was still. The footsteps paused at the corner, then continued down Traders Passage, then stopped. Her curiosity thoroughly aroused, the woman waited up to hear these footsteps night after night, with her companion, a charming young girl of twenty, for company. Both women always heard the footsteps, but they saw nothing. They turned on the lights of the house, flashed their torches into the road, but no person, nothing was ever to be seen. In spite of everything they tried, the mystery, it appeared, was likely to remain unsolved.

Then, eight years afterwards, in 1942, German bombs fell near Traders Passage, destroying several houses and bringing down parts of the retaining wall. A workman, a Corporation employee, cleaning away the rubble, found what he thought was a black bead necklace, took it home with him and gave it to his young daughter, aged nine. One day a stranger, who was a London jeweller, stopped the little girl in the street and asked if he might examine her necklace. Next he asked the child to take him to her father. To the father the jeweller explained that the necklace was composed not of beads but of black pearls. He bought it from the workman, took it up to London where, it is said, the pearl necklace was recognised as one lost centuries ago by a member of an English noble family which had helped to provide ladies-in-waiting to Queen Elizabeth. So perhaps the necklace was lost by a maid-of-honour who came with Queen Elizabeth to the ancient town of Rye in 1573; and perhaps the poor soul is at last at rest, now that her necklace has been found and restored, as has been reported, to one of her descendants.

Reysons Farm is a typical old Sussex farmhouse situated some six miles distant from Rye upon the Broad Oak–Udimore road. The house lies upon a ridge in country as lovely and historically interesting as any in England; for centuries this corner of East Sussex verging on the Romney Marsh was subject to the overlordship of the Norman Abbot of Fécamp. Reysons Farm is a taking example of its period and must have been a farmhouse since the sixteenth century, when the existing house was probably built. But there is said to have been a house upon the site since 1297. I have been hospitably entertained at Reysons Farm by the present farmer-owner, Mr. S. J. Holloway, who is also the author of a book, *Ancient and Modern Building*, and who has shown me round the intricacies of rooms, landings, doors and passages, as well as pointing out two framed coins dated 1675 (Charles II) and 1806 (George III) found respectively when digging to put in a new floor in the sitting-room and renovating an upstairs ceiling in 1950. Neither Mr. Holloway, nor any of his family, have ever experienced any uncomfortable atmosphere or manifestation of the supernormal at Reysons. There does, however, exist an unhappy legend that a very long while ago three people had lived there in a form of partnership to farm the land, two men and the wife of one of them. The husband died. Thereupon, the other man cheated his widow out of her share and cast her from her home with no money or possessions!

It is from my friend Mr. George Bullock, F.R.G.S., a previous owner of Reysons Farm (1942–1946) that I have the strange story that follows. When Mr. and Mrs. Bullock first went to Reysons early in 1942, they were told of hauntings which took the form, at infrequent intervals, of the sound of heavy footsteps climbing the back staircase, and then continuing along the passage; sometimes into the main bedroom, sometimes returning down the staircase and out again by the back door. There are two staircases in the house; the stories of hauntings seem always to relate to that which starts near the back door and connects with the bedrooms. The passage, or landing, passes by two subsidiary bedrooms, through the main bedroom, by another two rooms, after which it connects up with the second staircase leading to the lounge hall, that was previously the kitchen. From this meeting point an old door marks the entrance to steps up to the great wool loft. The loft in days long gone by provided a sleeping place for tinkers or other accepted wanderers who claimed a night's hospitality from the farmer. Mr. Bullock told me that variants of these reported hauntings hinted at the quality of curiosity on the part of whatever caused the sounds, for the footsteps had been known to stop outside the room where a stranger to the house was sleeping. "It" then tapped sharply upon the door as if to attract attention. What might have been seen had the stranger inside the room opened the door, remains unknown for there is no record of such a happening. But upon one occasion, it has been related, a guest staying in the big bedroom both heard the footsteps and saw a figure standing at the foot of the bed. Mr. Bullock wrote this to me in a letter: "The sound of the footsteps I heard once myself, but only once; but whether as a result of knowing the story, or because of the existence of some definite presence, I do not know. By the same token I always felt ill at ease in that part of the house where this staircase was situated. I incline to the belief that 'Something' was there, for the atmosphere of this part of the house was heavy and brooding; imagination would not be for me a satisfactory explanation." Mr. Bullock went on to relate a specific incident told to his wife and himself by a friend of the previous owner of Reysons Farm as an experience of her own. The time was immediately prior to the outbreak of war in 1939. I have altered nothing.

"One afternoon when she was upon a visit to Reysons, the owner—and her host—telephoned to say that his sister (I think that it was his sister, as far as my memory goes) had met with an accident and had been taken to Tunbridge Wells hospital. He said that he was going to see her and would not be home until late. His guest, whom I will call Mrs. Y, was to make herself at home but not to wait up for him.

"Mrs. Y, then, spent the remainder of the afternoon and the evening alone in the house. She was not in any way nervous—she had often stayed at Reysons. Anxious, she certainly was, but solely on account of the accident and how serious it might prove to be, not because she was alone in the house.

"The evening passed pleasantly enough until in due course, at around 11 p.m. she decided to retire to bed with a book. Before she went upstairs, however, she prepared a tray of sandwiches which she left upon the table in the kitchen, with a note. Mr. X could not fail to see these when he came in late and if, as she suspected, he was tired out both emotionally and physically, the food would be most welcome.

"Mrs. Y lay in bed reading for a long while. Finally, as the clock in the dining-room downstairs struck midnight, she decided not to stay awake any longer. She switched off her bedside lamp and went to sleep. Or tried to sleep, but without much success for nagging at the back of her mind was the worry of what news Mr. X would bring back with him from the hospital.

"When Mrs. Y had lain awake for some time, she heard the sounds of someone moving about in the kitchen at the foot of the stairs; then of footsteps mounting the staircase.

"She hurriedly switched on her lamp again and got out of bed. As she reached for her dressing-gown, the footsteps had passed the top of the stairs and were approaching her door. She called out in her anxiety for news:

"'Jack! How is Marie?'

"To her surprise, there was no reply. She heard the steps pass her door and continue along the passage. It is curious in a way that no thought of their being caused by a possible burglar occurred to her; she accepted unquestioningly that this was her host, arrived later than he had expected.

"Mrs. Y opened the door and called out again. Still there was no reply. The man had passed around the corner of the passage and was crossing the big bedroom. Feeling very angry by this time she hurried along after him, calling out yet again:

"'Jack! You are a pig! *What* is the news of Marie?'

"Still no reply, and she reached the door of a small bedroom beyond, which he used as a dressing-room. She could hear the footsteps again quite plainly inside the room. She rapped impatiently upon the door and again made her inquiry. There was no answer.

"She waited for several seconds and knocked again. When this produced no more result than before, she returned to her own room almost in tears.

"The following morning Mrs. Y went downstairs early to make tea as she usually did when staying at Reysons Farm.

"It was with a shock that she saw her tray upon the table, and her note propped up against the coffee pot, exactly as she had left them the night before.

"Within a short while her host came into the house, tired and unshaven. He told her that he had stayed at the hospital all night and had that moment returned from Tunbridge Wells. His sister was no longer in danger."

Chapter Seven

The Cheltenham Ghost: Mrs. Gaskell's Ghost Story, And A Spanish Coda

READING a life of David Hume, the eighteenth-century philosopher, the other day, I came upon the following sentences from "On Miracles" included in his *Essays Concerning Human Understanding*, 1748: "A miracle may be accurately defined, a transgression of a law of nature by a particular volition of the Deity, or by the interposition of some invisible agent.... No testimony is sufficient to establish a miracle, unless the testimony be of such a kind that its falsehood would be more miraculous than the fact which it endeavours to establish.... When anyone tells me, I immediately consider with myself, whether it be more probable that this person should either deceive or be deceived, or that the fact, which he relates, should really have happened. I weigh one miracle against another." Hume's test, to call it that, was intended for the miracles claimed particularly by the Roman Catholic Church, but I think it has equal validity in cases of psychical manifestations.

THE CHELTENHAM GHOST

I shall now tell the story of the Cheltenham Ghost (or the "Morton" Ghost as it was called before the ban on using the real names of those involved was lifted) at some little length, because it remains, perhaps, the best accredited ghost on record. This is an authentic ghost for all time, whose case was carefully investigated by the poet and philosopher Frederic W. H. Myers, then Honorary Secretary and one of the Founders of the S.P.R., who often stayed at his mother's house close to the haunt and questioned the witnesses at the time that the ghost was actually appearing. The results of his investigation were published in the *Proceedings* of the S.P.R. (Vol. VIII) under the title "Record of a Haunted House." This record is available to the general public as Appendix I in a recent book, *The Cheltenham Ghost*, by Mr. B. Abdy Collins, the late editor of *Psychic Science*, who examines the evidence thoroughly, both in relation to other ghostly manifestations and also with reference to the bearing of apparitions and ghosts upon the evidence for survival. Although, naturally, there has been much written about the Cheltenham Ghost, it is to Mr. Abdy Collins's book that I am most indebted for the shortened narrative which follows. I have included this extraordinary case because I believe that the facts cannot be gainsaid; also for fear lest some of my readers may have missed such unusual testimony.

The basic miracle was this—that in the 'eighties of last century a "female" ghost haunted for a number of years a house, built only twenty years before, in a fashionable part of Cheltenham. It was easily identified as the second wife and widow of the first tenant of the house, and was frequently seen by many people both by night and in broad daylight, not only in the house but in the garden. It seemed so real that it was usually mistaken for a living person by those who saw it. A daily contemporary record of the phantom's appearances was kept in a diary, copies of which were sent day by day to a reliable friend living in the north of England. Signed statements were taken from the chief observers by Frederic Myers himself. The point about this ghost is that it appears to have been a genuine spectre or phantom which haunted a definite place for a considerable period of time, and was there to be seen by anybody who happened to be present, provided that he or she possessed the faculty of seeing ghosts. It was, therefore, evidently something quite different from a personal or subjective "apparition" seen by an individual with whom it is concerned, such as the apparition of a friend, or relative, seen before or at the moment of death.

The house was built in 1860 and was then known as "Garden Reach"; but since that time its name has been changed twice and today, as St. Anne's, it is the Gloucester Diocesan House and stands in Pittville Circus Road, while All Saints' Road runs down one side of the garden. In the 'eighties it was described as "a typical modern residence, square and commonplace in appearance, separated from the road in front by railings with high gates and a short carriage sweep." Mr. Abdy Collins comments: "The house is so ordinary and modern and the garden so clear of trees and shrubs and in the front so open to the view of anyone passing along the road or living in houses opposite that it might seem incredible that not only was the house itself haunted but the ghost itself walked about in the front as well as the back garden and seems actually to have been seen there in broad daylight by persons totally unconnected with the family living in the house."

While yet unfinished, "Garden Reach" was bought from the builders by a Mr. Swinhoe, an Anglo-Indian, who lived in it for about sixteen years. "During this time in the month of August, year uncertain, he lost his wife to whom he was passionately attached and to drown his grief took to drinking.

"About two years later, Mr. S. married again. His second wife, a Miss I. H., was in hopes of curing him of his intemperate habits, but instead she also took to drinking, and their married life was embittered by constant quarrels, frequently resulting in violent scenes. The chief subjects of dispute were the management of the children (two girls and either one or two boys, all quite young) of the first Mrs. S., and the possession of her jewellery, to preserve which for her children, Mr. S. had some of the boards in the small front sitting-room taken up by a local carpenter and the jewels inserted in the receptacle so formed. Finally, a few months before Mr. S.'s death, on the 14th July, 1876, his wife separated from him and went to live in Clifton. She was not present at the time of his death, nor, as far as is known, was she ever at the house afterwards.

"She died on the 23rd September, 1878, and her remains were brought back to the town to be interred in a churchyard, about a quarter of a mile from the house in which she had lived." She had reached the age of forty-one years. The cause of death in her death certificate is given as being "Dipsomania 3 months: Subacute Gastritis 1 week." It was the ghost of this lady, Imogen Swinhoe, it seems certain, which haunted "Garden Reach."

After Henry Swinhoe's death his affairs were found to be much involved, and the house was sold to an elderly gentleman who, having had the house thoroughly cleaned and refurbished, for it was very dirty, went to live there with his wife of about his own age; but this was only for about six months for he died suddenly, by a rather curious coincidence in the same small sitting-room in which Mr. Swinhoe had died and where the jewels had been hidden, but in which the ghost was never seen. His widow moved into a smaller house, whether because of any experience or rumour of haunting is uncertain, and "Garden Reach" remained unoccupied for about four years. The landlord seems to have lived in it for three months and declared that he had never seen anything unusual. But is a landlord's word always to be trusted? Frederic Myers heard several second-hand stories, one about an old jobbing gardener, who worked for the house opposite, having often seen a tall lady in black in "Garden Reach" garden; but Myers was never able to substantiate such hearsay. However, it is known that for a period the house could neither be let nor sold, though it was on the market at about half the usual rental. It is only with the letting of the house in April, 1882, to Captain Despard, whose tenancy lasted for ten years or more, that the real story of the haunting begins.

Captain Despard's family consisted of his wife, described as "a great invalid," who like her husband never saw the ghost although she is said, along with her third daughter and the servants, to have heard "inexplicable noises and the sound of feet apparently going along the passages and up and down the stairs"; a married daughter, Mrs. K., of twenty-six (Mr. Abdy Collins thinks that the ages given may be for the middle year of the haunting, i.e., 1885), who was only an occasional visitor, sometimes with, more often without her husband; four unmarried daughters, Rose aged nineteen, Edith aged eighteen, and L. and M. who were fifteen and thirteen years old; and two sons, one of sixteen, who was absent during most of the haunting, and Willy aged six. Of these ten persons, five never saw the ghost, even though it may have been pointed out to them by those who did. Myers obtained further evidence from two of the servants and another witness who had played with Willy as a small boy.

But the principal witness is Rose Despard, who saw the figure often during the seven years 1882–1889. Very fortunately she kept a journal which she sent regularly to her friend, Miss Catherine M. Campbell, then living in the north of England, who, in a record sent to the S.P.R., testified that she had heard the footsteps, although she did not see the ghost. Frederic Myers referred to Rose Despard as "a lady of scientific training, now preparing to be a physician," and it is from her account that I must quote, selecting as much incident as limited space will allow me.

Rose Despard moved, with her family, into the house in April, 1882, but it was not until June that she had her first sight of the ghost, of which she had heard nothing, and noticeably she does not record any sign of alarm:

"I had gone up to my room, but was not yet in bed, when I heard someone at the door, and went to it, thinking it might be my mother. On opening the door, I saw no one; but on going a few steps along the passage, I saw the figure of a tall lady, dressed in black, standing at the head of the stairs. After a few moments she descended the stairs, and I followed for a short distance, feeling curious what it could be. I had only a small piece of candle, and it suddenly burnt itself out; and being unable to see more, I went back to my room.

"The figure was that of a tall lady, dressed in black of a soft woollen material, judging from the slight sound in moving.

The face was hidden in a handkerchief held in the right hand. This is all I noticed then; but on further occasions, when I was able to observe her more closely, I saw the upper part of the left side of the forehead, and a little of the hair above. Her left hand was nearly hidden by her sleeve and a fold of her dress. As she held it down, a portion of a widow's cuff was visible on both wrists, so that the whole impression was that of a lady in widow's weeds. There was no cap on the head but a general effect of blackness suggests a bonnet, with long veil or a hood."

A few facts about the figure may here be given. All those who saw it agreed that "it was opaque and so life-like that at first they mistook it for a living person." The outlines were "very distinct and the whole appearance solid." The phantom's attitude was always the same, with the right hand holding a handkerchief concealing the mouth, the left hand almost hidden by sleeve and dress. It was observed from the front, from both sides, and from behind. It sat at a writing-table in the drawing-room, walked in the garden in sunlight, looked in at the window. Occasionally it reacted to its environment, as in a strange incident recorded by Edith Despard: "The next time I saw the figure was one evening at about 8 o'clock, in July, 1885, a fine evening and quite light. I was sitting alone in the drawing-room singing, when suddenly I felt a cold, icy shiver, and I saw the figure bend over me, as if to turn over the pages of my song. I called my sister, who was in another room. She came at once, and said she could see it still in the room, though I then could not." So Edith saw the figure at first, but failed to see it directly afterwards when Rose did so! The first time Rose addressed it, it appeared about to speak but "only gave a slight gasp and moved towards the door." Six months later it behaved in a similar manner.

One of the oddest features was the way in which the figure was mistaken for a living person. Once the charwoman, while the family were at tea, was standing by the garden door waiting for her pay. She "saw a lady pass by, rather tall, in black silk, with white collar and cuffs, a handkerchief in her hand and a widow's fall." She had heard about the ghost but said "it never struck me

"*The figure was that of a tall lady, dressed in black of a soft woollen material, judging from the slight sound in moving.*"

that this figure could be a ghost—it looked like an ordinary person."

Another curious thing, more people heard the ghost than saw it. Footsteps, up and down the stairs and along the passage, were described as "very characteristic and not at all like those of any of the people in the house ... soft and rather slow, though decided and even." Whenever Rose Despard heard the footsteps and left her room to investigate she saw the figure. Rose recorded a queer feeling of loss, "as if I had lost power to the figure." On one occasion the two youngest girls saw "what looked like the flame of a candle without any candle or hand holding it, cross their room diagonally from door to door." There were thumps and knockings at bedroom doors; and handles were sometimes turned. The parlourmaid's bedroom door-handle was once "twisted right round as if someone was trying to enter" and she was terrified into a slight stroke.

All the same it seems certain that the figure was but a wraith that could neither be touched nor confined, and which passed through physical objects at will. Rose Despard put this to the test. "In May and June, 1884, I tried some experiments, fastening strings with marine glue across the stairs at different heights from the ground"; but she saw the figure pass through the strings without knocking them down. "I also attempted to touch her, but she always eluded me. It was not that there was nothing there to touch, but that she always seemed to be *beyond* me, and if followed into a corner, simply disappeared." Rose thought that the figure was seen by the family's two dogs. She describes how the Skye terrier apparently saw someone in the hall, ran up and jumped up as if expecting to be caressed. Then it "suddenly slunk away with its tail between its legs and retreated trembling under the sofa."

The limited period of the haunting (if we do not insist that the ghost was seen before the Despards moved in; for although this is probable, there is no first-hand evidence) was from 1882 to 1889, after which, though footsteps were heard occasionally, the figure was no longer seen. Unless, that is, we accept the evidence of an anonymous lady correspondent to Mr. Abdy Collins, who claims to have seen the ghost in the twentieth century, in the front garden in 1903. She says, further, that the house was later occupied by a Boarding School for Boys, "which eventually had to leave it owing to constant trouble from the ghost." Mr. Abdy Collins suggests that the limited but definite period of the haunting of "Garden Reach" by Imogen Swinhoe, together with the concentrated haunting during the years 1884 and 1885, followed by the gradual fading out in the next three or four years, is perhaps unique. In 1884 and 1885 the apparition was frequently seen all through each year, but especially during the months of July, August and September, which, says Mr. Abdy Collins "*may* be explained by the fact that Mr. Swinhoe died on July 14th, his first wife in August and Imogen herself on September 23rd. The alleged appearance of ghosts is often associated with the date of their deaths and there is nothing unusual in Imogen Swinhoe appearing more frequently in these months." He also makes the interesting point that had the haunting occurred today, "a competent medium would have been taken to the house and in all probability the 'ghost' would have been convinced of the futility of frequenting the scenes of her earthly life and the haunting would have ceased abruptly."

But how do we know that the phantom was the ghost of Imogen Swinhoe? Well, the identity of the ghost seems fairly clear when we take into account that there was only one deceased widow who had lived in the house and that she was Mr. Swinhoe's second wife, Imogen. The ghost was never seen anywhere but in the house, whose history was known, and in the garden, and all the witnesses agreed that it was dressed in widow's clothing. Also the figure is said to have resembled that lady and to have shown a partiality for the drawing-room, the room Imogen Swinhoe used most, and to have gone to the corner where she used to sit. "In fact," writes Mr. Abdy Collins, "the figure behaved exactly as Imogen Swinhoe might have been expected to behave if there are such things as earthbound spirits and she herself was earthbound."

In an earlier chapter I had occasion to quote the late Sir Charles Oman, formerly Chichele Professor of Modern History at Oxford

University, on Berry Pomeroy Castle. Sir Charles was also interested in Psychical Research and had been lecturing to the Oxford Psychical Society not long before his death. An account of this lecture, which he read in the Journal of the S.P.R., suggested to Mr. Abdy Collins that Sir Charles had some first-hand knowledge of the facts of the Cheltenham haunting, and a correspondence followed. What is interesting and significant here is the stress which Sir Charles places, in a letter to Mr. Abdy Collins dated May 9th, 1946, upon the mental agony endured by Mrs. Swinhoe, when alive, from her husband, sufficient perhaps to have caused an obsessional neurosis strong enough to have produced the haunting. I will conclude this case by quoting the relevant portion of Sir Charles Oman's letter:

"Yes, I know all about the Despard haunting but not so much from their point of view as from that of the ghost.

"My mother was a resident in Cheltenham and I frequently stayed with her. She was a friend of Mrs. S. and knew all about the tribulations from her dipsomaniac husband, who was a retired army surgeon if I remember aright. The wonder was that she endured his violent fits so long—she had a long bout of absolute danger from him. After his death she had something like a breakdown and finally left Cheltenham. She did not survive very long and did not die in the house where she had been so unhappy.

"I barely saw any of the Despards who took the house.... It was some little time after the Despards moved in that the story of the house and garden being haunted by the unquiet spirit of Mrs. S. began to get about Cheltenham. Frederic Myers, an old friend of mine, got on to the story. Like myself he had a mother resident in Cheltenham; indeed, she was a next-door neighbour to my mother. Hence much talk, but it was Myers who got on to the case and talked it over with me.

"The haunting seems to have died down gradually and was forgotten by all but a few."

Another Victorian ghost story, which for me has the ring of truth, is related by Augustus Hare in his second volume of *The Story of My Life*. It is a personal experience of Mrs. Gaskell, who wrote *Cranford*. Reminiscing about the year 1860, Augustus Hare writes: "The society of Mrs. Gaskell the authoress was a great pleasure during this term at Oxford. I made great friends with her, and we kept up a correspondence for some time afterwards. Everybody liked Mrs. Gaskell. I remember that one of the points which struck me most about her at first was not only her kindness, but her extreme courtesy and deference to her own daughters. While she was at Oxford, the subject of ghosts was brought forward for a debate at the Union; she wished to have spoken from the gallery, and if she had, would probably have carried the motion in favour of ghosts at once." He then reports her experience:

"Mrs. Gaskell was staying with some cousins at Stratford-on-Avon, who took her over to see Compton Whinyates. On their return she stayed to tea at Eddington with her cousins—cousins who were Quakers. Compton Whinyates naturally led to the subject of spirits, and Mrs. Gaskell asked the son of the house whether there were any stories of the kind about their neighbourhood; upon which the father, who was a very stiff, stern old man, reproved them for vain and light talking.

"After tea Mrs. Gaskell and her cousins went out to walk about the place with the younger Quaker, when the subject of the supernatural was renewed, and he said that their attention had lately been called to it in a very singular manner. That a woman who was a native of the place had many years ago gone as a lady's maid to London, leaving her lover, who was a carter, behind her. While in London, she forgot her carter and married someone else, but after some years her husband died, leaving her a large competence, and she came back to spend the rest of her life in her native village. There she renewed her acquaintance with the carter, to whom, after a fortnight's renewal of courtship, she was married. After they had been married a few weeks, she said she must go up to London to sell all the property she had there, and come down to settle finally in the country. She wished her husband to go with her, and urgently entreated him to do so; but he, like many countrymen in that part, had a horror of London, fancied it was the seat of all wickedness, and that those

THE CHELTENHAM GHOST

who went there never could come back safe: so the woman went alone, but she did not return. Some time after her husband heard that she had been found in the streets of London—dead.

"A few weeks after this the carter husband was observed to have become unaccountably pale, ill, and anxious, and on being asked what was the matter with him, he complained bitterly, and said that it was because his wife would not let him rest at nights. He did not seem to be frightened, but lamented that his case was a very hard one, for that he had to work all day, and, when he wanted rest, his wife came and sat by his bedside, moaning and lamenting and wringing her hands all the night long, so that he could not sleep.

"Mrs. Gaskell naturally expressed a wish to see the man and to hear the story from his own lips. The Quaker said that nothing could be easier, as he lived in a cottage close by; to which she went, together with five other persons. It was like a Cheshire cottage, with a window on each side of the door, and a little enclosure, half-court, half-garden, in front. It was six o'clock in broad summer daylight when they arrived. The door was locked and the Quaker went round to try the back entrance, leaving Mrs. Gaskell and her friends in the enclosure in front. They all, while there, distinctly saw a woman, of hard features, dressed in a common lilac print gown, come up to the latticed window close by them on the inside and look out. They then saw her pass on and appear again at the window on the other side of the door, after which she went away altogether.

"When the Quaker appeared, unsuccessful in opening the back-door, they said, 'But there is someone who could have let you in, for there is a woman in the house.' They tried unsuccessfully, however, to make her hear. Then they went to the adjoining cottage, where the people assured them that the man was gone out for the day, and that there could not possibly be anyone in the house. 'Oh,' said Mrs. Gaskell, 'but we have *seen* a woman in the house in a lilac print gown.' 'Then,' they answered, 'you have seen the ghost: there is no *woman* in the house; but that is *she*.'"

Although the subject of this book is English haunted houses, it is, possibly, well to remember that ghosts, if they exist, exist in all countries and climates.

An account of an exceedingly striking happening in Spain at the close of last century has, most kindly, been sent to me by Major Patrick Grant. The scene of this uncanny episode was Gibraltar, which is, however, still British!

Major Grant is the descendant of an old Highland family, with more than seven hundred years of recorded history behind it. He declares that he ought, therefore, to be credulous and superstitious, but does not believe that he is any more so than others, even in Scotland. And that, anyhow, the twenty-five years of his life as a soldier in the British, Indian, and African forces, let alone lately the armies of Finland and Czechoslovakia since 1939, ought to have knocked a good deal of easy credulity out of him. He says that for the following true happening, which he personally witnessed in his own early life, neither he, nor anyone else who has heard it, can supply an explanation:

"During the 'nineties when I was quite a young subaltern, I had obtained a 'spot' of leave and went out to Gibraltar to join my father and mother there for a fortnight or so. My father's regiment, the 42nd 'Black Watch'—and incidentally mine too at a later period—was quartered there and my father had very recently taken a house to live in when I came.

"It was very old, and for the purpose of this story I must give you an idea of it in some detail.

"Imagine a long, low house parallel with the road, from which it was separated, *and* secluded, by a very high brick wall, and set some twenty feet back. Between it and the wall was only a lawn of short grass, with no cover for a rabbit.

"Curiously, the garden gate into the road was opposite one end of the house, while the front door was exactly at the other end. The path led up to the window of the end room, past the windows of two other rooms, and to the front door which opened into a small hall. At *both* ends of the garden was an iron railing some six feet high, topped with spikes. Consequently, anyone coming to the front door had to pass all the windows on the way there and had to do so again when leaving.

"Stairs led from the hall to the ground-floor, which was paved with stone and which was below the level of the garden. Gibraltar, as everyone knows, is built on a slope and the ground-floor rooms had windows facing the *other* way and looking out towards the Bay. The walls were enormously thick. Two wells, one in the kitchen, the other in the only passage leading to the rooms, luckily were boarded over, for they were some forty feet deep. On that floor were numerous odd openings like small caves, which contained nothing and led nowhere; even niches in the thickness of the walls cut out for no known reason.

"The communication between these lower rooms was out of the passage. But the top rooms, from the hall to the last one nearest the garden gate, had intercommunicating doors from end to end of the whole house.

"My father and mother, myself, and my mother's English maid, had only just got into the house, which had been vacant for many years, and were still in the process of getting straight.

"One morning between 12 o'clock and 2 p.m. on a bright and sunny day I was in my room, which happened to be the end one opposite the garden gate. Something caught my eye and I saw an old Spanish woman who, apparently, had that moment entered the garden, for the gate was shut. She passed my window towards the front door, and I called out to my mother to tell her. She replied, 'Oh—yes. I'll tell Meadows (the maid). She has just passed my window.' I heard my mother tell the maid to go to the front door and, through the open communicating doors, heard the maid go and open the front door. There was dead silence for a moment, and then the maid said, 'But there's no one here, Madam.'

"I thought this odd, because I had continued to look out through my window and no one has passed *back*. Then my mother asked me if the Spaniard had gone out of the gate again and *how*, because from the moment she had passed the angle of the window on the way to the front door she apparently disappeared.

"I even opened my window and peered out in case the Spaniard was standing right up against the wall of the house—but *no*, the garden was empty.

"Naturally at that time in the day no one ever thinks of ghosts, and we came to the conclusion that both my mother and I had imagined we saw the Spanish woman.

"Two days later, about the same time, it so happened that my mother was in my end room and I in the room nearest the front door. My mother called out to me and said, 'There is an old Spaniard just inside the gate—I know why—your father asked someone to come to talk Spanish to him.' 'Right,' I said, 'he has just passed the window. I'll tell him father is out until later on.' I went to the front door, opened it, and there was no sight of a human being from one end of the garden to the other. I called out to my mother, asking if the man had gone out again; but she said, 'No.' 'Mistaken again I suppose,' we said, 'but it's *very* odd.'

"As it happened we were all three dining out with friends that night and there were some dozen or so people there. I was sitting on the opposite side of the table at dinner to that occupied by my mother. During a momentary lull in the conversation, a man on my side leant across the table and said, 'Oh, Mrs. Grant, did you know you were occupying the most famous haunted house in all Southern Spain? Have you seen the ghosts yet?' My mother replied, 'No—I'd love to, I am not the least frightened of them. What are they like?'

"But as the man began to describe what both my mother and I had seen, she begged him to stop and asked our host if she might have two pieces of paper and two pencils. These were brought; and then my mother asked for the description of the ghosts to be written on one piece, while she wrote on the other what she and I had seen. Amid intense interest on the part of everybody, these two pieces of paper were passed down the table to our host. He read first one, then the other—they were almost identical! My mother then requested the story of the ghosts. It went as follows:

"Nearly a century ago the house was occupied by a very wealthy Spaniard who had two servants, man and wife, in his employ. One day he went on a journey into Spain, leaving his servants to look after the house. Shortly after his return he summoned the servants and accused them of stealing a large sum of money and some jewels that he had hidden away in the house before leaving for Spain and which had disappeared. The servants swore their innocence, but he would not believe them and they were sent to prison for a long term. Indeed they died there, still swearing their innocence and saying, as they had continued to say, 'We will return and return again and again, even when we are dead, and find that money which *we* never stole.'

"After that no Spaniard would ever stay the night in the house; and, indeed, our Spanish cook and maidservant absolutely refused to live there, coming in daily instead. Of course our English maid knew no more about all this than we did! For days afterwards my father tried to find some kind of explanation for what we had seen, placing mirrors in different positions so as to see if the reflexions of people walking along the road were ever reflected into the garden or on to the window panes. But never a sign of result.

"Shortly afterwards the regiment left for Egypt, and I for England; and to this day I can *not* give any rational explanation of what my mother and I saw during the noons of those two days. As they used to say in the old days of 'Bridge,' 'I leave it to you, partner.'"

Chapter Eight

Evil Hauntings

PERHAPS the most mentally terrifying ghost-story in literature is *The Turn of the Screw*, and Peter Quint fiction's most evil ghost, because of that miasmal sense of the spreading breath of corruption which Henry James is able to convey. But after all, either symbolically or realistically, such literature is nearly always a reflection of life and of the dominion of death, and sometimes of the border states in between. In earlier chapters I have already suggested that many hauntings spring directly out of evil, as it were generated by crude violence, and producing a bizarre legacy of horrible vibrations enough to freeze the blood! I have reserved this chapter for some short, ghastly stories, the plain results of murder or atrocity; or which have in them much of the fantastic, macabre and abominable.

Therefore I will ask the reader's indulgence for the inclusion of such a story sent to me by Major Patrick Grant, which happened in India and should, perhaps, be outside the province of this book. Major Grant admits to having had "an infinite interest in stories," and tells me that, as he had the ability when he was young for learning languages easily, especially those of

India and Africa, he was always ready to listen to natives. Indeed, he confesses that he took more interest in the tales they told, once they knew that he would *not* laugh at them, than in the ordinary pursuits of soldiers in their profession or when "on leave." "By about 1906," he writes, "I had been transferred to the Indian Army and was with a local regiment composed of half Mers and half Merats who, of course, were the local inhabitants of that part of Rajputana, quartered in Ajmer, one of the oldest cities in all India.

"A few miles away from our cantonments was a steep hill crowned with a half-ruined fort many hundred years old which I noticed no native would ever go near.

"With that curiosity of mine I began to ask questions of not only my men, but also of the local people. I was told that the fort was haunted by the ghost of a dancing-girl which appeared on the anniversary of her death by flogging by the then local Raja who had caught her flirting with some of his courtiers. After a bit of questioning, I found out the approximate date and year, which was away back in the days of the Mogul Emperors, about 1500.

"The Raja had subsequently been killed and the fort had been an empty ruin from those days to this.

"When the date was almost due I managed, after sundry drinks in the Mess, to induce a brother officer, a fellow subaltern called Evans, to come and spend the night with me in the fort.

"As there were quite a number of panthers and hyenas in those hills, we armed ourselves with rifles and shot-guns. We took revolvers too, and in addition what, in India, is called a 'Bobbery Pack'—namely, a collection of some eight dogs of all sorts, including two bull-terriers whose courage we could rely upon in *any* event. Taking, too, some 'grub,' whisky, etc., two camp chairs and so on, we started towards evening of the day I had discovered was the right one. But even our soldier orderlies would not come into the fort and we had to cart the stuff ourselves over the last quarter mile or so. We dumped everything in the half-ruined room I had been told was the one in which the tragedy had taken place. We lit the lamps and made up a fire on the stone floor and sat down to await events.

"A few miles away from our cantonments was a steep hill crowned with a half-ruined fort many hundred years old . . ."

"The dogs lay at our feet and dozed and the night came along, but the lamps gave plenty of light.

"For hour after hour nothing happened and we both of us nearly went to sleep. But quite suddenly every dog awoke, their hair stood up stiffly on their necks and backs and all eight of them gathered together softly growling.

"We naturally thought of panthers and grabbed our rifles; but instead of looking towards the broken doorway, the dogs formed a sort of semi-circle looking at one corner of the room. Very, very slowly they advanced towards it, stiff-legged and seeming to be *dragged* there against their wills. Then their heads began to move slowly from side to side as if watching something we could not see. All the dogs moved as one and were gradually drawing nearer and nearer to the corner. Eventually they had formed a half circle round the corner from wall to wall.

"My limbs had stiffened, my throat was contracted. Quite frankly I felt a coward—something near to naked fear. I know my hand shook so much that I couldn't have hit anything even if I had seen anything to shoot at.

"As they drew nearer the corner the head of every dog moved less and less, until each gaze was fixed upon something—what?—that was in the corner itself. And then, in that dust of centuries, a movement caught my eye *below* the point where the dogs' gazes were fastened. The dust was turning in little whorls as if stirred by hands or feet—yet, though I strained my eyes as hard as possible I could see nothing but that dust turning round and round in little circles. Soon it was but one circle turning slower and slower: then all movement seemed to cease and the dust whorl settled down flat and motionless.

"It was some moments before my friend and I spoke a word. We were half congealed with horror. 'Did you see it?' I said. 'Yes,' Evans replied, 'the dust moved. Let's go—that's all I ever want to see.' 'Same here,' I said.

"At the sound of our human voices the dogs turned towards us, and the hair on their backs and necks went down. But they returned to us with their tails between their legs, looking not foolish as dogs do when they know they have made asses of themselves, but still utterly terrified. We patted them back to sanity again.

"After we had both gulped half a tumbler-full of neat whisky, we grabbed our things and went and we didn't go slowly. We almost ran down that hill and said nothing except 'good night' when we got back to our cantonments. Nor did we talk about it afterwards, or mention it to our brother officers for we knew they would laugh at us.

"But I, as ever, talked it over with my men the next day, for I knew they would not laugh.

"'Yes, Sahib,' they said: 'That was the story which has come down through all these centuries. It is why none of us go near the fort even in day-time and would never, never stay a night there. The girl tried at first to captivate the Raja, but she did not succeed in doing so. Then she stopped dancing and instantly the Raja flogged her with a bamboo cane, ordering her to go on dancing—"You shall go on dancing, and will dance to me till you die," he said.

"'And every time the girl stopped through fatigue he flogged and flogged her to her feet again until, in the end, she fell dead in that very corner where you, Sahib, saw the dust move.

"'It was her feet that stirred it: you could not see her, but the dogs did.'"

Yet it is not always the ghosts of the wretched victims, but sometimes the ghosts of the deceased criminals themselves that appear. In England there is reason to believe in the reputed ghosts of several notorious murderers, one of which was not quite a straightforward ghost because he operated his malignant haunting through his own severed skull! Mr. Thurston Hopkins—a famous ghost-hunter, who dates his interest in psychic phenomena back to about his tenth year when his family was living in the governor's house within the walls of the old prison at Bury St. Edmunds in Suffolk—told me this true story of the Murderer's Skull, and how it brought misfortune to his father and to his father's friend, while I talked with him at his house in Brighton. His father had bought the disused Bury Gaol and turned it into a home, so that as a child Mr. Hopkins must have literally played round a gallows. He remembers being much impressed by a black-framed faded letter in a murderer's handwriting, the last confession of William Corder, who murdered Maria Marten in the Red Barn at Polstead. It is easy to think of "The Murder in the Red Barn" as a popular and sensational past melodrama, forgetting that the murder really was committed and Corder hanged for it.

Mr. Hopkins's father, who used to tell this tale after supper on Christmas night, spoke of ghosts as if they had always been accepted by all sensible people. He was as certain of their existence as his scientific friend, Dr. Kilner, was sceptical, having, he boasted, scant time for "all this tomfoolery about ghosts." Yet for many years the doctor's family had been linked with the Red Barn Murder, and Dr. Kilner had been bequeathed some gruesome relics—the pickled scalp and tanned skin of Corder—by the will of a former surgeon at Bury Gaol. Then many years after the hanging Dr. Kilner removed Corder's skull from the skeleton, wiring a spare anatomical skull in its place, and had the murderer's cranium polished and enclosed it in a square ebony box which was placed in a cabinet in his drawing-room. But from the first moment, he admitted afterwards, he had felt uncomfortable about "something" and had to close his mind to an uneasiness that overcame him.

After surgery hours a few evenings later, the servant told him that a gentleman had called to see him: "Proper old-fashioned looking he is—he's wearing a furry top hat and silver buttons on his blue overcoat." Rather reluctantly the doctor went to see. There might have been someone there by the window, it was dark... but when the maid followed with a lamp, the caller had vanished.

A week passed, when again one evening the doctor saw, through his drawing-room window, a stranger lurking by the summer house, who was wearing a beaver hat and an old-fashioned coat. He vanished as the doctor was about to step out.

The haunting had begun. At night doors opened, voices muttered, the servants complained of sobbing and hammering in the drawing-room. Nobody could sleep. The doctor was forced to believe that the Skull was trying to plead with him. He would have liked to have returned it to the body of the murderer, but its highly polished condition would have made this impossible without detection. The haunting went on.

Then one night some noise woke the doctor. He got out of bed, lit a candle, and looked over the stair-rail: he saw the glass knob of the drawing-room door, reflecting the light, now suddenly blotted out by a hand. There was a white hand, but no figure. The knob began to turn, the door was stealthily opening. Suddenly the doctor was almost knocked down by a big explosion. Fury seized the sceptic. Full of loathing for the skull he never should have tampered with, he rushed to the drawing-room to be met by a terrific gust of wind—or was it a huge menacing form enveloping him? His candle went out. He lit a match; he saw a grinning malevolent Skull, with the wreckage of the black box shattered into a thousand pieces all over the pale Indian carpet.

Dr. Kilner gave the skull to Mr. Hopkins, with the remark: "Take it as a present. As you own Corder's condemned cell, and the gallows where they hanged him, perhaps it won't harm you to look after his skull."

But it did. As he was carrying the skull away in a handkerchief, Mr. Hopkins twisted his foot and was temporarily bedridden. The same day his best mare broke her back. Next illness swept through the household. Within months both Mr. Hopkins and Dr. Kilner were nearly bankrupt.

So Mr. Hopkins decided he must break the evil spell of the skull. He took it to a country churchyard and bribed a gravedigger to give it Christian burial. After that both men prospered. His son is insistent that this story is not an invention, that names, places and facts are correctly stated and can be verified.

For cold wickedness and devilish cruelty Mrs. Amelia Dyer, the Reading baby-farmer and the murderess of nobody knows how many infants entrusted to her care, whose tiny corpses were fished out of the Thames and other rivers at the latter end of 1895, was one of the most nauseating old hypocrites in the history of crime. While her evil deeds were being brought home to her at the Old Bailey, she clasped a hymn book, sanctimoniously, in the dock and had to be prevented from leading the court in prayer.

In his *Ghosts Over England* Mr. Thurston Hopkins narrates an episode of how Mrs. Dyer came back to haunt Chief Warder Scott at Newgate Prison after she had been executed on June 10th, 1896. Chief Warder Scott said that Mrs. Dyer broke his nerve when she was alive and haunted him when she was dead. "It wasn't that she was a troublesome prisoner," he said, "she was too submissive and oily for words. But her eyes were always watching me, and her hands folded on her black dress. . . . Those glittering eyes of hers instilled into me a strange feeling of disquiet and foreboding. . . .

"At that time the Keeper of the Old Bailey had a blue-and-white English setter dog, and he had left it in my charge during his absence. The dog hated Mrs. Dyer from the start and I know why—it was the faint, sickly reek which issued from the woman. It reminded me of the odour of ancient marshlands under a strong sun. The dog always cowered past her cell with tail drawn in and head abased. Dogs can smell cruel people I am certain!" This statement is interesting to compare with the behaviour of the dogs in the Indian fort.

It is said that just before Mrs. Dyer walked from her cell to the execution shed she looked at Scott: "I'll meet you again some day, sir," she said. The rest is best told in Mr. Thurston Hopkins's own words:

"One night just before Newgate was closed down for good several of the warders were having a bottle of whisky together to celebrate the final week of duty in the prison. They were sitting in the Keeper's room next to the Women Felons Yard. There was a door with a glass observation wicket looking out to the yard. Suddenly Scott felt aware that someone's eyes were fixed on him, and he heard a voice ringing in his head: 'Meet you again . . . meet you again some day, sir.' . . . Then he looked towards the door and Mrs. Dyer's face was framed in the grille. There was no mistaking her oily benevolent smile, the little dark, snake-like eyes and the thin lips trying to look kind and harmless.

She gave Scott one sad enigmatical look and passed on. Scott jumped up and opened the door and saw nothing except a woman's handkerchief which fluttered at his feet on the wet flagstones.

"There was no woman convict in the prison at that time—indeed the reception of women prisoners had been discontinued for some years."

Touching upon the subject of evil hauntings, Cardinal Newman said this: "We cannot doubt that evil spirits in some way are always about us; and I had comfort in the feeling that whatever was the need, ordinary or extraordinary, I should have protection against it.... How can people say what is or is not natural to evil spirits? What is a grotesque manifestation to us may not be so to them. What do we know about an evil spirit?" Poltergeists apart, there are a few rare stories concerning ghosts which harm, but none of them matches in horror the grisly belief in vampires, probably still held in some remoter parts of Eastern Europe. The best English vampire story, printed by Augustus Hare in *The Story of My Life* and reproduced by Charles G. Harper in his *Haunted Houses*, might be called "The Vampire of Croglin Grange," which house was supposed to lie in Northumberland, but I do not feel there is reason to tell it here. Krafft-Ebing, in his *Psychopathia Sexualis*, connects the vampire legend with sadism; and D. H. Lawrence found in Poe's tales a symbolical and mythological translation of the "thirst for unrealizable love and of the desire for that complete fusion with the beloved which ends in vampirism." Therefore, believing that vampires have more to do with the limits of erotic romanticism than with genuine hauntings, I will say no more about them.

However, W. T. Stead in his *Real Ghost Stories* offers us a ghost capable of inflicting physical injury which "not only strikes the first blow, hitting a man fair in the eye, but afterwards sets a ghostly dog upon his victim and then disappears." This story was sent to Stead by the Rev. Henry Kendall, a Congregational minister in Darlington and a painstaking and persevering collector of such matters. The narrative was signed by the protagonist, Mr. James Durham, on December 5th, 1890, and is as follows:

"I was night watchman at the old Darlington and Stockton Station at the town of Darlington, a few yards from the first station that ever existed. I was there for fifteen years. I used to go on duty about 8 p.m. and come off at 6 a.m. I had been there a little while—perhaps two or three years—and about forty years ago. One night during winter and about mid-night or 12.30, I was feeling rather cold with standing here and there; I said to myself, 'I will away down and get something to eat.' There was a porters' cellar where a fire was kept on and a coal-house was connected with it. So I went down the steps, took off my overcoat, and had just sat down on the bench opposite the fire, and turned up the gas, when a strange man came out of the coal-house, followed by a big black retriever. As soon as he entered my eye was upon him and his eye upon me, and we were intently watching each other as he moved on to the front of the fire. There he stood looking at me, and a curious smile came over his countenance. He had a stand-up collar and a cut-away coat with gilt buttons and a Scotch cap. All at once he struck at me, and I had the impression that he hit me. I up with my fist and struck back at him. My fist seemed to go through him and struck against the stone above the fire-place, and knocked the skin off my knuckles. The man seemed to be struck back into the fire, and uttered a strange unearthly squeak. Immediately the dog gripped me by the calf of my leg, and seemed to cause me pain. The man recovered his position, called off the dog with a sort of click of the tongue, then went back into the coal-house, followed by the dog. I lighted my dark lantern, and looked into the coal-house, but there was neither dog nor man, and no outlet for them except the one by which they had entered.

"I was satisfied that what I had seen was ghostly, and it accounted for the fact that when the man had first come into the place where I was sat I had not challenged him with any inquiry. Next day, and for several weeks, my account caused quite a commotion, and a host of people spoke to me about it; among the rest old Edward Pease, father of railways, and his three sons, John, Joseph, and Henry. Old Edward sent for me to his house and asked me all particulars. He and others put this question to me, 'Are you sure you were not asleep and had the nightmare?' My answer was quite sure, for I had not been a minute in the cellar and was just going to get something to eat. I was certainly not under the influence of strong drink, for I was then, as I have been now for forty-nine years, a teetotaller. My mind at the time was perfectly free from trouble.

"What increased the excitement was the fact that a man a number of years before, who was employed in the office of the station, had committed suicide, and his body had been carried into this very cellar. I knew nothing of this circumstance, nor of the body of the man, but Mr. Pease and others who had known him, told me my description exactly corresponded to his appearance and the way he dressed, and also that he had a black retriever just like the one which gripped me. I should add that no mark or effect remained on the spot where I seemed to be seized.

(Signed) James Durham."

The alarming experience of the night watchman was investigated as thoroughly as possible at the time. In various letters to W. T. Stead, the Rev. Henry Kendall made his comments upon the case:

"Mr. Durham has attended my church for a quarter of a century, and I have testimony going back that length of time to the effect that he has given the same account of the extraordinary experience. It is a long time since he retired from the post of night watchman, and he has since become a wealthy man. He is one of the strongest men I have met with, able to do his forty miles a day, walking and running with the hounds, and not feel stiff the day after. . . . I forwarded his strange narrative to Prof. Sidgwick, the president of the S.P.R., who expressed a wish for fuller assurance that Mr. Durham was not asleep at the time of the vision. I gave in reply the following four reasons for believing that he was awake: First, he was accustomed as watchman to be up all night, and therefore, not likely from that cause to feel sleepy. Secondly, he had scarcely been a minute in the cellar, and, feeling hungry, was just going to get something to eat. Thirdly, if he was asleep at the beginning of the vision, he must have been awake enough during the latter part of it when he had knocked the skin off his knuckles. Fourthly, there is his own confident testimony. I strongly incline to the opinion that there was an objective cause for the vision, and that it was genuinely apparitional. At the same time I see that it was shaped and coloured to some extent by the percipient's own temperament, as apparitions often are. Mr. Durham, with the habit of a watchman, when he sees anything in the least degree suspicious, is immediately on the alert, doubtful and inquiring till he obtains satisfaction; and it is significant that when the apparition entered the cellar they immediately eyed each other and continued doing so all the time, while the apparition moved on to the front of the fire.

"Again, Mr. D. is a believer in physical force, prompt, decisive, not disposed to brook any delay, but wishing a man to come to the point with him there and then; and it corresponds with the quality in him that the man all at once struck out at him, and that he struck back again, and that the dog gripped him, and was then called off and immediately retired with his master. It is the only instance which I remember in which an apparition attempted to injure, and even in this solitary instance there was no real harm done."

In a second letter Mr. Kendall wrote: "Today I have visited the scene of the battle with the ghost, under the guidance of an old official who was at the North Road Station during all the period in question. The porters' room down the steps is still there, and the coal-house and even the gas bracket. My guide remembers the clerk who committed suicide, and he showed me the place where he shot himself with a pistol. His name was Winter. He left a wife, but no children. He was no doubt in trouble, from which he fled by suicide. He dressed and had a dog as described. The explanation accepted by the stationmaster and men at the time was that Mr. D. had had a five-minutes' nap. This was, of course, a gratuitous supposition on their part, as they were not there, and Mr. D., who was, declares he was wide awake. Even if he had dozed, there would still remain the remarkable correspondence between what was seen and the habits of the suicide when living, and which were unknown to the percipient."

Three days later Mr. Kendall wrote again: "After looking at both sides, I must say the accuracy of Mr. D.'s account seems to remain unimpeached, though, of course, it is not evidential after the high standard of the Psychical Society. A strong, sober man is likely to know whether he was asleep or not at such a crisis.

"One objection has been made to this effect: Mr. D. had a cabin at the level crossing, and there was his post. What was he doing down in the porters' room at the station? But it was long since he left the crossing. For fifteen years he was watchman at the station and round about it, and during that time the porters' room was his proper place if he wanted to sit down by a fire and take some refreshment.

"The room is not used by the porters now. The station is homely and old-fashioned, but interesting as successor of the first that ever was, which was a few yards away across the Durham Road. The No. 1 engine, run on the day of opening with George Stephenson as driver, stands in front, exposed to wind and weather." Surely this interesting record deserves a place in all books about railways.

A friend of mine who lives in Tunbridge Wells has told me of a terrifying happening that occurred a long time ago in a fine mansion in Dorset. The mansion must remain anonymous. In 1941 he was entertaining some officers, from a heavy Ack-Ack battery, who were stationed at Southborough in Kent. The men were very young, my friend middle-aged and distinguished; in spite of the excellent sherry, the conversation was inclined to flag. Then one boy mentioned the mansion in Dorset, in which he said they had been billeted before coming to Southborough. His host jumped at this opening, for he knew the mansion. "I know it," he said. "It's a really beautiful place. That must have been extremely pleasant."

"Well, sir, it wasn't actually," said the young subaltern, going pink and stopping as though he felt embarrassed.

"Oh, why?"

"Well, sir, you'll probably laugh at me. We didn't like it. It was rather a bad show. You see the house was haunted."

"Indeed I shall not laugh at you! Please tell me what happened."

"I suppose it wasn't much really," the young officer replied, "but somehow we all got an odious, almost crushing sense of evil. The owner had had to turf out at forty-eight hours' notice and before we moved in he had removed, or stored, most of the art treasures—all except one picture of a mature woman over the mantelpiece in the dining-room. This painting, the owner had told our Colonel, must be left exactly where it was and on no account be shifted. Well, we had put a dart-board up beside it, and one evening during play the frame was chipped by a dart. The Colonel put us properly on the carpet. He said that a dart would pierce the woman next, and as the picture was almost certainly valuable he was going to take it down and store it. He did, and it was after that the trouble started."

"Do please go on."

"It doesn't sound very much. We used to lie in bed, with the black-out curtains drawn back, looking through the open windows at the stars. On moonlight nights the moon would shine into the bedroom and glint brilliantly upon the polished door-handle. We used to watch the door-handle turning and the door would open. We couldn't see anything, but there was a filthy sense of evil, and sometimes we almost felt we were being followed about. I'm afraid that's all, sir." The boy laughed uneasily. A fellow officer corroborated what he had said.

"I think," remarked their host quietly, "that I may perhaps be able to throw a little light upon this. By an odd coincidence during the first war, in 1917, I was sent down to recuperate in Dorset and stayed with an elderly lady in that exact neighbourhood. This lady knew all the local history and told me, what many people believed, that your mansion had once been the scene of a tragedy.

"Isn't it rather queer how history repeats itself? In 1806, or thereabouts, a Regiment was quartered near-by against the threat of Napoleon's invasion. The General was asked to dine at your house, his host requesting him to bring along with him a cornet as there was to be quite a big party, with dancing afterwards. While dinner was in progress the General, to his consternation and amazement, saw the young officer, whose parents were known to him, behaving in a most unnatural and rude manner. Although he was seated between two pretty and attractive girls, the officer was taking absolutely no notice of them, but was staring with an expression of fixed, unmitigated horror at the face of his hostess who sat beside the General at the head of the table. The General, anxious and growing angry, tried by coughs and frowns to bring the boy back to his proper senses.

"Suddenly the cornet, with a cry of 'I can't bear it!' pushed back his chair, rose, and rushed Macbeth-like from the feast! The General immediately followed, thinking that the boy had gone raving mad; mounted his horse in the courtyard, and galloped after the diminishing hoof-beats of the young officer's horse. But the General gradually gained ground, and at last drew level and caught hold of the runaway's horse's bridle. 'Now what in the name of hell?' the General shouted.

"'In the name of hell, that's it!' gasped out the cornet. 'I tell you I saw a hooded figure standing close behind her and you, and it was *willing* her to commit suicide!'

"'Nonsense, nonsense, my boy!' But at that moment the hoof-beats of a third horse were heard. The rider approached at break-neck gallop. He drew rein, a footman wearing the livery of the house.

"'Where in God's name are you going?' cried the General.

"'To fetch a doctor,' the man answered. 'But, alas, I fear it is too late. Just after you both left, Madam picked up a table-knife and cut her throat in front of everybody.'"

Five miles north of Arundel, built on a chalk ridge of the majestic South Downs, Amberley today is still one of the loveliest and most sequestered of Sussex villages whose thatched and whitewashed cottages, with their little flower gardens, and its old church and castle, call more to mind the quiet beauty modestly immortalised in the paintings of Edward Stott than crime and ghosts. Yet something tragic, pitiful and violent must have happened here during the reign of Queen Victoria; for there seems no doubt at all that Amberley Vicarage used to be haunted by the ghost of a little girl. I went down to Amberley to investigate and was shown over the vicarage.

EVIL HAUNTINGS

I had read a short story by Miss Noel Streatfeild called "The Little Girl" in the *Evening Standard* on May 18th, 1955, and had been struck by its ring of truth. Miss Streatfeild, who confirmed that the story was true, has generously permitted me to draw upon the incidents contained in it. Her father (who went on to become Bishop of Lewes) was given his first living at Amberley in 1897. She was a very small child when she lived in Amberley Vicarage, and her subsequent knowledge of what happened was told her by her parents as she grew older. As with so many country children who look back, she remembers the vicarage garden best because walking in it was often a great adventure, especially when she shared a rose tree with another girl-child who was not one of her three sisters. Noel never met this little girl except in the garden, although an older sister saw her in the house.

Though the Streatfeild children took their odd companion for granted, they were secretive about her, never mentioning her to their parents. Nor did the parents ever speak about the little girl; the less they thought about her the happier they were. Although the vicarage possessed a spare bedroom, thanks to the little girl, and an adult who sometimes accompanied her, no relatives ever came to stay on a second visit.

Apparently, while nobody on either side of Miss Streatfeild's family had the power of seeing either the little girl or the adult woman with her, they were all uncomfortably conscious of the two strange presences. At night, as they watched, the bedroom door-handle would slowly turn, the door would open—they would feel the unseen child tip-toeing across the room, painfully sense someone peering at them. The relations' sufferings were increased by an enforced conspiracy of silence. Unable to bear the room's uncanny atmosphere, one guest was found to have left before breakfast the next morning! Sometimes the little girl would have naughty fits and throw crockery about; the noise of smashing china was heard in the kitchen. Still Miss Streatfeild's parents kept silent, hoping that by ignoring the manifestations sooner or later the house would return to normal. It never did. The Streatfeilds were forced to accept the unpleasant fact that to other people the house was "wrong." Nobody would stay with them. Much as he loved the village, the Rev. W. C. Streatfeild was delighted when he was offered another living.

Almost at once after the arrival of the new vicar, the Rev. Dr. G. F. Carr, with his wife and family, the evidence for the reality of "the little girl" becomes more direct. Dr. Carr's daughter, Miss Irene Carr, who lives at Westham, Pevensey, has not only been kind enough to give me a verbal account of what her mother saw, but has found and lent me the original document written in her mother's hand-writing just after she had seen the apparition soon after they had moved in in 1902. I cannot do better than give a shortened version of this statement by Mrs. Ella Louisa Carr:

"One day in May I was sitting in my arm-chair resting after lunch, feeling very tired, when I happened to look out of the dining-room window and saw a little girl of about seven years old coming through the garden gate. She was dressed in a white cotton frock with short sleeves; her hair, which was parted in the middle, fell in thick fair curls each side of her face. As I sat lazily watching her, she opened the small iron gate leading from the outside path up to the house, and walked up to the door. I waited instinctively to hear the bell ring, but though I listened carefully I heard no sound. The servants at this hour—about half past two —were sitting in the kitchen having their dinner, and easily able to hear from that room the door bell ring. It is often the habit of village children to come up in this manner with messages, so I waited with some curiosity to know what this one had called for.

"Time passed and none of the servants brought me any message. At last I went to the kitchen door and asked what the child had come for. 'What child?' they said. 'No one has called.'

"So I explained to them about the little girl I had seen coming up the path, and described her appearance. They still maintained that they had seen no one, and that no one had rung any bell. . . .

"A few days later I was calling on a near neighbour, when as I was leaving I asked quite carelessly whether she knew if there were any visitors staying in the place. She replied, 'Oh, no, it is much too early in the year for visitors, but why do you ask?'

I explained about seeing the child, how she came to the door and no one had heard her ring.... I again described her and mentioned her white frock, curls and age. The lady then exclaimed to my great astonishment, 'Oh, don't you know. That's the Apparition.' 'Apparition,' I said, 'what Apparition? Nonsense, it was a flesh and blood child I am sure, and the only reason I asked you about it was that I knew it was none of the village children, and I thought you would know who was staying in the village....'

"Here I should like to mention that I am no believer in ghosts or apparitions, and when I saw the child, it was my firm opinion that it was an ordinary flesh and blood child.... I was told that, at long intervals, people living in the cottages had seen a little child dressed in the same manner appear in different rooms and houses. One woman said it sat on the end of the bed."

An old man was supposed to haunt Amberley Vicarage as much as the little girl. In fact, Miss Irene Carr told me that one of the Streatfeild children was reputed to have woken up one night screaming, "The old man! the old man!" This old man tramped up and down the stairs.

About the year 1904, while the vicarage was being rebuilt and modernised, the Carrs were living at Worthing and Dr. Carr used to go over to Amberley to take Divine Service. One Sunday he went into the vicarage to see if the workmen had found the papers which he thought "the old man" must have wanted. A workman told him, "We haven't found the papers, sir, but we've found the ghost!" Under a rough board in a cupboard in the dining-room they had laid bare two skeletons, one a woman's, the other a little girl's, which it was computed must have lain there about a hundred years. The Rev. Clarkson had occupied the vicarage for fifty-seven years before the Streatfeilds, and Mr. Clarkson had sometimes complained of an inexplicable smell in the dining-room. The Clarksons's cook vowed she had seen the old man walking, possibly haunting the scene of his crime for the haunting does seem to point to an illicit love affair, with, perhaps some years later, the murders of a discarded mistress and her child. In Dr. Carr's time his dogs often showed frantic terror in the kitchen, where more bones were found. Miss Irene Carr's brother once saw a blue light travelling across the landing and passing into a bedroom. Mrs. Ella Louisa Carr's written statement continues:

"At the end of the room in which I had been sitting when I saw the Apparition, an old wall had to be pulled down in order to lengthen and enlarge the dining-room. In digging out the foundation close to the side door a deep trench was discovered filled with earth of an entirely different colour and quality from the other parts. On digging down about two feet, a number of bones were found. These at first the workmen paid no attention to, until they found two skulls, which on examination proved to be those of human beings. One skull was that of an adult, but the smaller one was proved to belong to a child of apparently seven years of age, as shown by the teeth still remaining in the jaws. This exactly agreed with my observation of the age and size of the child I had seen.

"How the skeletons came there, or what their previous history was, remains a mystery still. When I saw the child I had never heard the legend of the Apparition, though we had often heard strange noises about the house to which we had paid no attention, none of us being believers in ghosts. . . . I offer no explanation of the above circumstances as I know of none."

It was decided to give the two skeletons Christian burial; but before the date arrived for the interment, some bones had been left lying about in accessible places. Though it may seem hard to credit, many detached pieces of bone were carried off by the village people as souvenirs. Dr. Carr buried such remains as were left. From that day of the burial to this the woman and the little girl have not been seen again.

Chapter Nine

The Remarkable Mongoose

"I CAN believe anything provided that it is quite incredible" is, of course, Oscar Wilde's. I wonder whether Wilde would have believed then the preposterous story of the Talking Mongoose, which seems at first sight so manifestly absurd? In the Isle of Man a cat without a tail is understandable; but here is a Manx tale that is not understandable either by logic or by reason, nor is it likely ever to be explained by the laws of our at present imperfect physics.

Nevertheless, for all its fairy tale oddity and almost childish appeal, this is a documented case to which such qualified men as the well-known American psychical researcher, Hereward Carrington, and the New York psychiatrist, Dr. Nandor Fodor, who when he first investigated it was Research Officer of the International Institute for Psychical Investigation (London), have given considerable puzzled credence. Dr. Fodor's view is recorded in *The Story of the Poltergeist Down the Centuries*, which he wrote in conjunction with Hereward Carrington. The other source of my necessarily abbreviated account must be *The Haunting of Cashen's Gap* by the late Harry Price and

R. S. Lambert. Mr. Lambert at the time he helped to probe into this "modern 'miracle'" was editor of the B.B.C. weekly, *The Listener*. He was deemed crazy for believing in the Talking Mongoose by Sir Cecil Levita, a former chairman of the L.C.C., and forced into bringing an action for libel on account of his position at the B.B.C. After a sensational trial, he was awarded £7,500 damages.

The story is nothing less than the claim that an animal, which haunted a lonely farmhouse in the Isle of Man, really talked, where, says Dr. Fodor, "all probabilities are against it, but all the evidence is for it." My motive for including the career of the remarkable mongoose in this book is that Gef, whether regarded as fact or fiction, undoubtedly was both spirited and amusing. Following so many tragic, grim hauntings, the reader may, I hope, find Gef's antics a relief, a welcome change.

Doarlish Cashen—Manx for Cashen's Gap, a gap in the hedge —is an ancient, bleak and remote farmhouse, built of slate slabs faced with cement, out of sight of any other farm, perched about seven hundred and twenty-five feet above sea-level upon a treeless, shrubless slope of Dalby Mountain on the west coast of the Isle of Man. A little grey porch projects, sheltering the front door from gales. The interior architecture is unique, because when Mr. James T. Irving bought Cashen's Gap in 1917, he had an inner wall of dark match-boarding added to keep out the draughts. The commodious space between these boards and the walls, communicating with a low attic which runs right across the cottage, would provide an ideal hiding-place for a small animal wishing to remain an invisible companion of the family. Also there were plenty of peep-holes from the ceiling into the bedrooms, as well as from the match-boarding into the living-rooms. Out of doors fields of long uncut grass, with high sod-hedges cutting off the view, would again make it easy for a small animal to trail human beings without itself being seen.

During the four years of the mystery of the "man-weasel" (late 1931 until late 1935), as the "Manx prodigy" was first called by the Press, the interior of Cashen's Gap has been described as

"Doarlish Cashen . . . is an ancient, bleak and remote farmhouse . . ."

dark and rather eerie, with its low ceilings and the matchboarding stained almost black, and the living-room lit at night by a small paraffin hand-lamp. But the house was more comfortably and tastefully furnished than one might have expected in such surroundings. There were chairs, a cushioned sofa; a gramophone; and pictures showing an interest in other countries, a tattooed Maori chief and street scenes in Istambul. The fact is that Irving was no ordinary simple Manx farmer, but an educated man, with some knowledge of the world and a smattering of other languages. He had been a commercial traveller, representing a Canadian firm of piano manufacturers, and he knew German and had also picked up phrases of Russian, Arabic, Yiddish, even Hindustani. He was a non-smoker and abstemious in his habits. At this time he was a white-haired, healthy, cheerful man in his early sixties, who tended his forty-five acres of rough grass and gorse and this thirty sheep which, with a few goats and some poultry, were the mainstay of his farm. He had once been prosperous, but the farming slump after the First World War had hit him, and now he was forced to live very frugally indeed. Irving was a vigorous man who enjoyed life and did not shun his fellows. Both he and his wife had won a high reputation throughout the island for sincerity and honesty. However, he seems to have been autocratic in his family circle. Dr. Fodor has written about this: "A withering look that shot out of his eyes like a bolt of lightning silenced them very effectively when they felt like contradicting him."

Mrs. Irving, Manx on her mother's side, has been called by Price and Lambert "clearly the mainstay of the Irving domestic establishment" and depicted in terms of admiration. "Mrs. Irving, to outward eye the most striking personality in the household. You see a tallish woman of fifty-nine, of dignified bearing, upright and square of carriage, neatly dressed in the style of a former generation. Her grey hair rises primly above her forehead, to frame her most compelling feature—two magnetic eyes that haunt the visitor with their almost uncanny power. Mrs. Irving belongs to a type that you would guess at first glance to be 'psychic'; she herself believes firmly in her own powers of intuition, and has gifts of seeing more than ordinary mortals see with the outward eye.... Like the rest of her family, she is well-spoken and well-informed."

Then there was Voirrey (Manx for Mary) Irving, born in 1918, a mere child when Gef first made himself known, seventeen at the close of the mystery, the period of her adolescence. Was Gef, then, a poltergeist attached to the young daughter of the house? It seems not, because poltergeists are malicious and wicked, which Gef was not; and poltergeists are nearly always invisible, while Gef claimed to be solid flesh and blood, with fur and teeth. He ate food put out for him and drank and coughed and performed his natural functions. Nevertheless, at first Voirrey seems to have been the central attraction for Gef, who acted as her guardian, though his affection spread later more evenly to the whole family. He made himself useful by killing rabbits—he strangled them— and told where they could be found; for rabbits were an important item in the modest larder at Doarlish Cashen.

Although Voirrey had a much older brother and a married sister, they were away and do not come into the story. She was in effect brought up as the "only child" of elderly parents and gives the impression of having been somewhat jealously cherished, but not of being soft; she was isolated, without friends; rather reserved, silent and self-possessed. She grew into a tall, well-built girl, with fair hair coiled in plaits about her ears and a rosy outdoor complexion. Her photograph shows her with eyes half shut and a rather disdainful expression. It is recorded that, like the rest of her family, she shunned bright sunshine which seemed to hurt her greenish-brown eyes that carried something of her mother's strange look.

Voirrey was always the first of the household to be up, making tea for her parents, milking the goats, and doing other chores; and on most days she tramped the downs with Mona, the brown collie sheep-dog, picking flowers or mushrooms or bilberries, and inspecting the rabbit-snares set the night before by her father. Sometimes, while Mona mesmerised a free rabbit to immobility, she would creep up behind and kill it with a sharp blow upon the neck. Voirrey was uninterested in books, unless they dealt with animals; but she also had a passionate interest in things mechanical such as cameras, motor-cars and aeroplanes. Her character was not without feminine vanity. For visitors she would wear a silk or cotton frock, a necklace, a gold signet ring; she used perfume, but not lipstick.

It may be conceded that the Irvings were a cheerful, united, and healthy trio of averagely intelligent people. But, reading the accounts, it does strike one that the parents were probably somewhat jealous and over-possessive about Voirrey. When Harry Price and R. S. Lambert offered the girl a free holiday in London, her parents refused to let her go. Once when Harry Price, "believing that the phenomena originated in Voirrey's pubertal upheaval, wanted to have a private conversation with her and invited her for an automobile ride," Irving was indignant. Dr. Nandor Fodor, who would appear to look partly to the psychology of the father for a solution of the mystery, makes this comment: "It was an innocent enough request from a middle-aged man in whom an uncultured farmer girl hardly could have evoked passions. But Irving refused point-blank. As he told me the story, he grew red in the face and shouted: 'If Harry Price wanted a girl, he should look for one elsewhere.' The rage probably served another, ulterior motive; it covered up the fear that Irving would lose the central role in the drama of the Talking Mongoose."

How did the mongoose, or whatever it was, first come to Cashen's Gap? While Dr. Fodor never solved the mystery of the Talking Mongoose, he avers that he learned more about it than all those who visited the farmhouse before him. He spent a week at Doarlish Cashen as a guest of the Irvings, and this is what Mr. Irving told him of the marvellous opening happenings in September 1931:

"One evening we heard a noise: tap, tap, tap. The noise came from the attic which is boarded in. I thought we had mice. The following day I opened up the ceiling and found a little Indian wood-carving, which I recognised as my own. How it got into the attic I cannot tell. When I dropped it, it produced the same type of sound as we heard the night before.

"That evening the sound came again, but this time louder. Then it became a running noise. 'That is no mouse,' I said to my wife. I was right. We heard animal sounds: barking, growling, hissing, spitting and blowing. This was followed by a crack that shook the place and sent the pictures on the wall swinging.

"It was plain that an animal had got into the house, but the crack was a mystery. I did not think that an animal could make that sound. Soon I had to stop thinking. Something happened which made us speechless with marvel and apprehension: the animal was making gurgling sounds like a baby when it begins to talk. . . .

"This was followed by a bark with a pleading note in it. I was amazed. I repeated the noises of various animals: vow-vow—dog, meow—cat. Back came the same sound and the human word for it in a shrill and high-pitched voice, issuing from a very small throat.

"I was carried away with wonder. An animal was taking lessons from me in human speech! It was too amazing to be true. Yet, in a few weeks' time 'he' spoke fluently, using all our words and lots of others. There was incessant questioning and a prodigious thirst for knowledge. 'One more question, Jim,' the voice used to plead, 'then I will let you go to sleep!'" Gef told them that for years he had understood everything that people said, but that he could not speak until he was taught. In 1932 Mr. Irving thought that Gef might be an Indian mongoose, because some twenty years earlier a farmer in the neighbourhood had procured and released a number of mongooses in the fields to kill rabbits. But later Gef said that he was not a descendant of these, but "that he was born on June 7th, 1852, and came from Delhi and had been chased and shot at by natives!"

In those first alarming days a state of war existed between the farmer and Gef, and Mr. Irving confessed to feeling afraid. "What in the name of God can he be?" he whispered to his wife; and then Gef would throw the very words back at him, for nothing escaped the ears and watchful eyes of the animal. Was he a ghost? Gef encouraged this belief, until he was certain of his reception. "I am a ghost in the form of a weasel, and I shall haunt you with weird noises and clanking chains." Yet he wanted to be friends and alternately pleaded for acceptance and threatened. "If you are kind to me, I will bring you good luck. If you are not kind I shall kill your poultry. I can get them wherever you put them.

"I am not evil. I could be if I wanted. You don't know what damage or harm I could do if I were roused. I could kill you all if I liked, but I won't." But Gef had a habit of throwing all sorts of things into the room with great force, and, who knows, he might one day throw a knife! So Irving tried to hunt him with a gun, and then to kill him by poison. Gef eluded all attempts at capture either dead or alive. In the beginning sometimes his language was so violent that Voirrey's bed was moved into her parents' room; they then thought the mongoose must be an evil spirit in animal form. Once Voirrey heard diabolical screaming behind the panelling, and Mr. Irving imagined that Gef must have eaten some rat-poison he had put down. The loud screaming went on for more than twenty minutes, reminding Irving of "a pig having its nose 'ringed'." Another time when the three Irvings were in bed, they were kept awake for half an hour by groans and sighs as if from someone in acute agony. When asked why he plagued them in this way, Gef answered: "I did it for devilment!" During the first months the Irvings seriously thought of leaving Cashen's Gap, so objectionable was the animal's behaviour. But he gradually grew better behaved, until he had become quite affectionate, showing alarm at any mention of the Irvings leaving the farm. "Would you go away and leave me?" Gef asked.

"Yes," said Mrs. Irving, "you have not helped us."

"I got rabbits for you."

"You promised to help us to make money, and you have not done so."

"No. If you make money, you'll go away and leave me." One night Gef admitted that he had three attractions in the house, saying: "I follow Voirrey; Mam gives me food; and Jim answers my questions."

What then was this remarkable mongoose like to look at?

Who actually saw him, or had tactile proof of his presence? The only visual evidence comes from the Irving family; yet Dr. Fodor maintains that "deliberate deception on their part over a period of years is unthinkable and does not cover the case." Collective hallucination, he points out, is extremely rare; only morbid or ill people suffer from it, and none of the Irvings were either. As for the charge of ventriloquism, this "is best answered by the fact that Gef has been heard when each member of the family has been alternately eliminated." In a reply to a letter from Harry Price sent on February 22nd, 1932, Irving wrote:

"The animal in question has been seen by myself and daughter of 14, in one of the two bedrooms of my house, on several occasions in the month of October last. My daughter has on two occasions in January 1932 seen its tail only, in the small back kitchen, in a hole in the wall. My wife has seen it on one occasion only in October. The colour is yellow, not too pronounced, after the ferret. The tail is long and bushy, and tinged with brown. In size, it is about the length of a three-parts grown rat in the body, without the tail. It can, and does, pass through a hole of about 1½ inches diameter. I, personally, am strongly inclined to the view that it is a hybrid between a stoat and a ferret. The bushy tail is not that of a stoat, and the size certainly half that of the ferrets I have examined.... My daughter says the face is all yellow, and the shape is more that of a hedgehog, but flattened at the snout, after the fashion of the domestic pig."

By all accounts this strange small creature, who described himself as "a little clever, extra clever mongoose," was very shy and nervous of being seen. For years he was most often just a voice, which those who heard it said was "shrill and high-pitched, one or two octaves higher than human speech." One night the Irvings saw his animal shadow cast by candle-light, and he had fingers, instead of claws, with which he could "pick up things and throw them." His fingers were once seen through a crack near the ceiling and were "short, yellow, and the nails curved." Later, Gef allowed his fingers to be touched. There were three on each hand and a thumb. Mrs. Irving was even allowed to stroke his fur and put her finger into Gef's mouth. "My long finger seemed to fill Gef's mouth," she told Dr. Fodor. "His teeth were tiny and sharp. He drew a little blood from my finger. I was indignant. I told him: 'I don't want any blood poisoning here.' He answered: 'Go and put ointment on it!' His mouth was about an inch wide."

While no human witness outside the Irving family will testify to having actually seen the mongoose, rather surprisingly and inconsistently because of his marked aversion to being seen, Gef did allow himself to be photographed several times. "I will have my photograph taken," he said, and Voirrey Irving made the attempts. Unfortunately none of the photographs are particularly good. In July, 1935 Voirrey was given a present of a new Kodak by Harry Price and R. S. Lambert, and the best picture she took (reproduced in *The Haunting of Cashen's Gap*) claims to show Gef on top of a sod hedge near the farm. Though it could well be the photograph of a small furry animal, as evidence I should say that it is inconclusive.

The aural evidence is much better, however, for Gef was heard to talk by various visitors outside the family, most notably by Captain Macdonald, the racing motorist, who was another investigator of the case. Alas, I have no room here to enter into details, but Captain Macdonald firmly believes he heard Gef; and so does Mr. Charles Northwood, a retired cotton broker and godfather of Voirrey Irving, and also his son Arthur. "Northwood," Dr. Fodor writes, "has been a close friend of Irving for thirty years and was ready to vouch for his absolute integrity.... By the end of his visit, Northwood was convinced that Gef was what he claimed to be: an animal. His son, Arthur, on the other hand was equally convinced that Gef was an earth-bound spirit.... Two boys, Harry Hall, aged nineteen, and Will Cubbon, aged fifteen, both of Peel" called at Doarlish Cashen and also witnessed that they had heard Gef speak. Harry said to Dr. Fodor:

"Mr. Irving told us that Gef can tell the head or tail of a penny if it is placed in the porch window. I took a penny from my pocket, tossed it and placed it on the window-ledge. As soon as I came back into the kitchen, Gef shouted: 'Tail.' He was right.

I tossed again. He was right again. The third time I did not toss. I left the penny as it was. Gef said: 'You did not turn the penny.' The voice was a very high, screechy sort. I never heard one like it. When Gef spoke, Voirrey was in the kitchen, Mr. Irving near the fireplace, Mrs. Irving sitting on the sofa. Neither of them could see what I was doing."

Gef was never, in a physical sense, a prisoner at Cashen's Gap and was free to come and go as he wished. The Irvings had no control over his movements; neither could they make him talk if he didn't feel like it. Sometimes he went away for days at a time. But there would seem to have been some curious psychic bond between him and Mr. Irving—something, could it have been, halfway between a Prospero-Ariel and a Prospero-Caliban attachment?—which was voiced in his pathetic, pleading cry of: "Jim, let me go, let me go." When Irving replied: "I am not keeping you, be off. Where are you going anyway?" the mongoose would answer: "Back to the underground. Vanished."

The animal would roam the countryside, enter people's houses quite unknown to them and, listening, pick up private gossip and disconcertingly bring back to the Irvings intimate knowledge. His "coo-ee" would sound from behind the sod hedges. Folk were uneasy. "That mongoose knows far too much," they said. He once threw gravel at the window of a lonely cottage out of mischief. "The female was hiding behind the door," he said. "Then Father came out with a whacking big stick." The childish side of Gef's mentality, his juvenile interest, is strongly suggested by the evidence of Will Cubbon. "He asked me: 'Can you drive a steamroller?' I said: 'Yes.' He did not believe: 'You young rascal, you would put it over the hedge.' He told us: 'Clear to hell.' Several times he said: 'I'll wet on your head.'"

Gef was especially fond of the word "hell." After paying a visit to a country estate twenty miles away, he volunteered that he had had "a hell of a job to climb over the wire net" which surrounded it. He had travelled under a lorry, he said: "Oh, God, was I tired!" When the Irvings, marvelling at his courage—he might have been seen, or killed by dogs—asked him how he dared do it, he replied simply: "I watch like hell!"

The Irvings believed that Gef gathered a great deal of his local information from hearing the talk of people in buses, under which he was said to hang and listen. Mr. Irving asserted that many times he had been able to verify absurd items of news that Gef had picked up and relayed to him. Hearing that the Talking Mongoose was stealing bus rides, "the electrician at the Peel bus terminus set up a contact plate under the bus to electrocute Gef. Irving heard of this and, being very fond of Gef, warned him. 'Oh, I know all about it,' he answered. 'It is under Bus 81.' Irving did not know this. He inquired and found that Gef's knowledge was precise."

But Irving declared that it grew increasingly hard to check up on Gef's statements, because people hated to be told that the Talking Mongoose had paid them a visit. Dr. Fodor found this out too. One final story. Gef claimed to have gone twice to a large mansion in the north of the island, which no member of the Irving family had ever visited, and had returned with much exact descriptive detail of the grounds and of the interior. Dr. Fodor writes: "I hired a car and travelled twenty miles to call on the owner. He was evidently nervous. He called me 'spooky man.' He wanted to prove Gef wrong. But as it happened, Gef's statements were 90 per cent accurate. He reported, for instance, that there was a fireplace in the house ornamented with lions. The owner denied this. But it appeared soon that he never had a good look at his own fireplace. Lion heads *were* all over the woodwork, and there was a small, full-size lion on top." Gef liked this house so much, saying that he had raided the pantry and that there was plenty of food there, that he threatened to leave the Irvings, to go away. But Dr. Fodor never believed that he would do so, because at Cashen's Gap the panelling and spy-holes suited him perfectly and because "he needed the Irvings to satisfy his craving for companionship." He seemed happy and laughed all day, titteringly, mischievously, sometimes satanically. Asked if one of the three Irvings had to die, which he would prefer, he replied: "I do not want any of you to die. I like you all, but don't let us talk about death!"

The complementary question of the affection, or otherwise,

that Gef inspired in the Irving family is an interesting one. At times he must have tried them indeed! As a young child Voirrey was fond of him, for he was a companion and shared in the games she used to play with the sheep-dog, Mona. He would watch her hide and call out: "She is not ready yet!" But later she cooled off and finally agreed with her mother that Gef was a nuisance and said she "would gladly be rid of him." Yet Mrs. Irving showed herself heartbroken once when Gef had been missing for nearly five weeks. She suspected he was still in the house. "Mrs. Irving's impassioned appeal to Gef to 'come out'," wrote Harry Price, "would have brought tears to the eyes of less hardened investigators than ourselves, and if she were merely playing a part—what a consummate actress!" Mr. Irving probably thought most kindly of Gef, was proud of the mystery, realising its potentialities for scientific investigation. He would certainly have regretted Gef's death by accident or his removal from Doarlish Cashen.

Finally, Dr. Fodor makes the point that Gef's character was quite unlike that of any of the three Irvings. He was by turns cheeky, obstreperous, jeering, threatening, pathetic, and brave. Whether fact or fiction, he lives as the surprising individual creation of somebody. Here, to close this fantastic, remarkable history, are a few of Gef's contrasted sayings:

"Hey, Jim, what about some grubbo?" Once, having helped himself from the meat-safe, he apologised to Mrs. Irving: "Maggie, I hope you don't mind, I have eaten the bacon." Another time he had seen through a spy-hole a box of chocolates that Captain Macdonald had sent to Voirrey. He was asked if he were hungry and he replied: "Yes, I will have some of Captain Macdonald's chocolates; a nut and a black paradise and a muck sweet!" He liked human food, not mongoose food. The farmer woke up one morning in April, 1932, to hear the animal crying: "Jim, Jim, I am sick!" and heard him vomit behind the panelling. It was found that he had stolen some carrots from a cottage eight miles away. Another time he complained of "joint evil" in his tail, a complaint common to foals, an expression he must have picked up on a farm. Evidently, he learnt his words from listening to people, and would ask Irving their meanings, with amusingly solemn affirmations: "Jim, what is 'countenance'? What is 'loco'? What is a 'nun'? Honest, Jim! Word of Honour, Jim!" Sometimes he showed quite a power of literary expression. He had spied on Irving reading the *Bible:* "Look at the pious old atheist, reading the *Bible*; he will swear in a minute." Ironically, and most amusing of all, Gef was afraid of ghosts. Irving told Dr. Fodor: "While sitting on the bed, I heard Gef talking to my wife and daughter below. I enveloped my head in a sheet, took off my boots and slipped noiselessly downstairs. As I entered the kitchen, Gef screamed with fright: 'Clear to hell.' When I took the sheet off, he sobbed like a child."

What then are we to make of all this, and how did the haunting end? It ended by the Irvings selling Doarlish Cashen and vanishing. There was a strange postscript in 1947. The new farmer-owner claimed to have shot a queer-looking animal like a mongoose, which he thought must have been Gef because, he said, the house was no longer haunted. But Gef might have died, or gone away with the Irvings. Nobody knows. Dr. Fodor maintains that "it is an incredible tale, but not a trumped-up one." That something called Gef existed and talked, he holds proved.

If so, what was Gef—a ghost, a poltergeist, a "familiar" from the world of witchcraft, an earth-bound spirit in animal form, or just "a little clever, extra clever mongoose"? I do not think that he was a "familiar"; although, since he admitted to having once killed the turkeys and four ducklings belonging to a man he didn't like, it seems probable that in an earlier century this would have been enough to have sent all three Irvings to the stake!

In his perplexity, at the end of 1932, Irving consulted a friend on the Liverpool Cotton Exchange, who told him that some Indian fakirs possessed the power of making mongooses speak. And there were those mongooses that had been released twenty years earlier in the district. We know that parrots, budgerigars, ravens and jackdaws can produce the sounds of human words. The problem narrows into a question of the possibility of the operation of an independent, speaking animal intelligence.

Dr. Fodor writes: "Remarkable animals are known to have existed before Gef. The Elberfeld horses could extract cube roots and communicate thoughts by striking, in code, with their hoofs. Dogs have been taught to read and spell. . . ." And did not the Lord open the mouth of Balaam's ass?

We may perhaps leave the last word to Dr. Fodor, who suggests that the root of the mystery might have been approached in the psycho-analytical exploration of Irving's unconscious mind acting upon an unusually developed animal brain. He thinks that Dr. Maxwell Telling of Leeds may have come close to the mark when he offered as a solution the theory that "Irving's unconscious somehow captured and 'obsessed' a precocious animal intellect, and while giving it every opportunity for personality organization, prevented it from escaping by reason of the outlet which it gave to his own frustrated self"; so that Gef "was a missing link between the animal and human intellect." Unfortunately, it seems unlikely now that the mystery of the remarkable mongoose will ever be solved.

Chapter Ten

Theatre Ghosts

LIKE Antonio I sometimes hold the world but as the world, seeing it as a stage where every man must play a part. In the theatre we find ourselves in a magic realm where millions of strange shadows tend on the actor. Here is the meeting-place of life and the arts; and such is the alchemy of art and the power of metempsychosis that we grow confused, uncertain as we watch which is the real world and which the more ephemeral. Tragedy has entered many a time into the life of some poor player who portrays the mimic scene before us. Art transposes reality, so that we are not quite sure what is shadow and what substance. If anywhere, here in the theatre, surely, there should be ghosts, born either mysteriously out of the creative pains and romantic sorrows of life or, more simply, from the impassioned brain of a master dramatist.

Theatre Royal, Drury Lane, one of the most celebrated theatres in the world, is undoubtedly haunted. We have evidence for that. It has been said to be full of ghosts, although not all of them can be vouched for. Nevertheless, there is one superior Drury Lane ghost—The Man in Grey—who has been seen by countless people and is the most famous of all theatre apparitions. He would seem to be harmless enough, never interfering with anybody; and he is a daytime ghost only appearing between the hours of 9 a.m. and 6 p.m., never at night. A quiet, courtly spectre in the form of a strong-faced young man of the handsome late Sir George Alexander type, he is just over middle height and wears a three-cornered hat upon either powdered hair or powdered wig, and a long grey riding-cloak of the early eighteenth century, beneath which can be seen riding boots and the end of his sword. Sometimes he carries his cocked hat, and is clearly visible unless one gets too near when he goes out of focus and vanishes. He walks purposefully and is never hurried, sometimes even during a matinée when the house is full, from one side of the Upper Circle to the other, disappearing through the wall. Whether one can see him or not will depend upon the possession, or otherwise, of that special sense to discern ghosts. But this phantom has been seen at Drury Lane by generations of men and women, and notably by that great historian of the London theatre, Mr. Macqueen-Pope who, in his book *Theatre Royal, Drury Lane*, writes that he "wishes to put on record that he has seen this apparition on numerous occasions." He tells in the same book how it was once seen by a charwoman who had entered the Upper Circle to start her work shortly after 10 a.m., while a rehearsal was proceeding on the stage:

"She saw, sitting in the end seat on the centre gangway of the fourth row, a figure of a man in grey, wearing a hat, gazing down at the stage. She thought it one of the actors, who had assumed his costume, but also thought she had better make sure. She therefore put down her pail and her broom and went to speak to the figure. As she neared it, it seemed to vanish, and then reappeared at the exit door on the right hand side of the circle, through which it passed. She imagined it was some trick of the eyes, this vanishing, so she did nothing about it, except to report it later. . . . She had never heard of the ghost before in her life, but gave a description of it which tallied accurately with all the others."

During a matinée of a big musical play not long before the last

Drury Lane: the Man in Grey.

war, records Mr. Macqueen-Pope, this ghost was seen by a lady playgoer in the Upper Circle, who asked an attendant if the appearance of actors among the audience was part of the show! She had seen "a man in a long grey cloak, with a white wig and cocked hat, pass through the entrance door just ahead of her." And again on an autumn evening in 1942 "Mr. Stephen Williams, Broadcasting Officer of 'Ensa' at the time, saw the ghost clearly whilst he was on the grand staircase near the upper circle entrance. Another 'Ensa' official said he saw it in the Green Room; but if so, this is its only recorded appearance backstage."

Mr. Macqueen-Pope, one of the busiest as well as one of the most knowledgeable men of the theatre in London, is never too busy to help a friend; so I heard personally from him his own likely theory of the possible explanation of the Man in Grey. Although there is no horror in the ghost—a recent offer to exorcise him was rejected with contumely by everybody at Drury Lane who regarded him as a mascot—yet there could well be a link between him and the most horrifying discovery ever accidentally made within the walls of a theatre.

It seems that Christopher Rich, that bad old cheese-paring manager of Drury Lane, who robbed his actors and was obsessed with making structural alterations to the house in order to squeeze in a few more seats, may even have been the unwitting origin of the ghost. The walls of a dark closet in a narrow passage had survived both the rebuilding of 1796 and the fire of 1809. Just over one hundred years ago, some workmen employed on the Russell Street side of the upper circle of the theatre came upon a portion of the old thick walls that sounded hollow. It was decided to break through that part of the wall and see what was wrong. What they found was very wrong—a small chamber which had been bricked up, and in it a male skeleton with a dagger in the ribs. There were bits of cloth with a corded edge that crumbled at a touch. The dagger was of a Cromwellian pattern, but it might have been a theatrical prop. The bones were buried in the little graveyard at the corner of Russell Street and Drury Lane, the cemetery mentioned by Dickens in *Bleak House*, where Lady Dedlock died. Mr. Macqueen-Pope's suggested solution of the mystery is that the victim of the murder may have been a well-to-do young gallant from the country, who came to town to cut a dash. He would naturally gravitate to the playhouse and no doubt invade the stage to show himself off. What more likely than that he became too friendly with one of the girls and that her lover either murdered him, or had him murdered, and hid the body in a small room which he knew was to be bricked up? Whoever he was, today he is a portion of the story of Drury Lane.

Moreover, casts of productions at "The Lane" have invariably liked this gentle theatre-loving ghost, for he is thought to bring them luck. He would appear to be a good advance critic, shunning failures, and most often seen before and during the production of a success. For he was seen within a week before the opening nights of such successful Ivor Novello musical spectacles as "Glamorous Nights," "Careless Rapture," "Crest of the Wave" and "The Dancing Years." After the war Drury Lane reopened with Noel Coward's "Pacific 1860" which failed —the ghost was never seen. But he revealed himself three days before the first night of "Oklahoma," two days before "Carousel," two days before "South Pacific" and three days before "The King and I" started their triumphant runs, and he was seen again several times during the lives of all these shows.

Other ghosts are alleged to haunt Drury Lane, but they are less easily authenticated. A tall, emaciated, hatchet-faced wraith said to stalk across the theatre in front of what used to be the pit, could be that quick-tempered Irishman Charles Macklin who, in 1735 during a quarrel in the Green Room over a wig, slew a brother actor, Thomas Hallam, by thrusting at him with a stick that pierced his eye. Curiously, Hallam has never been seen to walk. If the ghost is Macklin, perhaps he is doing penance for his crime.

Astonishingly circumstantial is the claim of an elderly lady from Birkenhead who, during the period of the Boer War, went with her sister and brother to a matinée of a Drury Lane Drama. Some years ago she wrote to Mr. Macqueen-Pope to tell him that she had seen a ghost, which was not the famous Man in Grey.

They had occupied three gangway seats in the old auditorium off the side block of the dress circle. The rows then ended flush with the walls, so that anybody entering their row would have had to pass them. Glancing along the row, the lady was more than surprised to see a man with longish hair, wearing very old-fashioned clothes of the early nineteenth century, sitting a few seats away. Her sister saw him clearly too, but her brother could not and jeered at his sisters for imagining things. For a while, after the curtain rose, the two women saw the man watching the play with interest. At the end of the act when the lights went up, they looked again—he was gone! Yet nobody had passed by them. In 1945, very soon after Mr. Macqueen-Pope's book, *Theatre Royal*, was published, he received a letter from this lady, saying that she now knew with certainty whom it was she had seen on that afternoon such a long time ago. It was Charles Kean, whom she had easily recognised from his photograph in the book, exactly as she and her sister had seen him.

Readers of Sir Osbert Sitwell's autobiography *Left Hand, Right Hand!* will remember the fascinating description of how Stanley Lupino, when playing in pantomime at Drury Lane, at "the hour of make-up" saw the face of that long dead, lonely, superb comedian, Dan Leno, reflected beside his own face in the looking-glass. Although, apparently, nobody else has received such a visitation, Sir Osbert Sitwell, writing of Dan Leno, avows: "As I have said, everything connected with him was unusual and moving, and I find the appearance of his ghost to the late Stanley Lupino—which he describes in his excellent book of memoirs—most credible.... Lupino learned subsequently that this had been the favourite dressing-room of Dan Leno, and the last he had used."

It was King Charles II who gave Drury Lane its Charter, so it is perhaps worth mentioning that there is a man who swears that on a summer afternoon in 1948 he saw the King, with a crowd of courtiers, revisit his Royal Theatre. They passed down the side gangway of the stalls, mounted the stage and joined the company of "Oklahoma."

We come now to a most curious, yet genuinely authenticated,

phenomenon, for an account of which I am once more indebted to Mr. Macqueen-Pope and his recent book, *Pillars of Drury Lane*—to a tactile ghost, a ghost of touch. There would appear to be theatre ghosts that reverse the behaviour of the model child in the Victorian nursery and are heard and not seen. For example, old J. B. Buxton, a dear kindly man in real life, haunts his former dressing-room at the Haymarket Theatre; but nobody has ever seen him, only heard him opening the door and walking in, rummaging in a cupboard, and shutting the door as he goes out. The St. James's Theatre, too, can claim a similar, but this time unidentified, tactile ghost in a dressing-room; since some people have felt themselves helped on with their coats, then the touch of a ghostly brush upon their shoulders—who knows, maybe this could be the spirit of some earth-bound "dresser"?

Returning to Drury Lane, many readers will remember that during the exceptionally long run of "Oklahoma" the cast often changed—almost every part had several players. A pretty, charming young American actress, Betty Jo Jones, had come over from the States to play the comedy rôle of "Ado Annie." She was somewhat inexperienced, still young in her profession, and had never before played in so vast a theatre or upon such a large stage. As is well known "The Lane" can be hard on comedians. In her first few performances Betty Jo Jones found she was not getting her scenes over the footlights as she wished, although she was playing the part precisely on the lines first laid down, which had by then become traditional. She failed to get her laughs and was eliciting little response from the audience. She was most upset, realising that she was not succeeding.

One night she was playing a scene in which two actors were on the stage with her. Suddenly she felt a gentle tug at her skirt. She looked round, but neither of the men, as the scene demanded, were near enough to have touched her. Now she was aware of two hands upon her shoulders, gently but firmly forcing her down stage and guiding her body into a new angle. She felt a friendly pat on the back. She played her scene from this fresh position and got the comedy over. Next night she had forgotten, but once again the ghostly hands guided her; she obeyed and received her applause. From the time she took the position indicated by her unseen helper, she had no more trouble. She called on Mr. Macqueen-Pope and told him her story. He listened to her with close attention, for he had heard rumours of this before. Betty Jo Jones wondered who the good-natured spirit could be, but she was positive about her experience.

The "Oklahoma" miracle was almost repeated. At the beginning of the production of "The King and I" a young actress, Doreen Duke, with a fine singing voice, had to attend an audition for a part which she was extremely anxious to play. She was apprehensive and scared; to sing to an almost empty, enormous auditorium is a considerable ordeal. As she passed on to the stage, like Betty Jo Jones, she was conscious of two hands upon her shoulders and a reassuring feeling of friendly guidance. She knew the same calming pat on her back when she had finished. She got the part. During rehearsals, on the first night, and occasionally afterwards, she was as sure as Betty Jo Jones had been of the occult help she was given. One theory suggests that the kind invisible mentor could have been Joe Grimaldi, the famous clown, who had a full knowledge of comedy, singing and drama, and made his final farewell from the stage of Drury Lane. Besides being a great clown, Grimaldi was a good soul who had always helped people in his lifetime; it would be in character that he should continue to do so after death.

Mr. Macqueen-Pope told me one gruesome tale of the Lyceum Theatre that occurred in the 'eighties of last century. A man and his wife sat in a box, watching the show, enthralled. In the first interval the man's gaze became fastened upon a woman, wearing flowing silks, who was sitting in the fourth or fifth row of the stalls, well away from the gangway. His eyes had caught something on her lap which looked like a man's head. His wife was staring too. He said: "What has that woman got on her lap?" His wife said: "It looks like a man's head!" The lights were just going down.

During the next interval the man and his wife descended into the stalls to try and get a closer look. But they were unable to get near enough, and if there had been an object it was now covered by the lady's silk wrap. They returned to their box. At the end of the play they tried to intercept the woman as she left her seat; but in the crowd they missed her. However, the face of the head remained fixed in the man's mind; it belonged to a head of the cavalier type, with long hair, moustache and pointed beard; it looked pallid, dead, as if beheaded.

The grisly episode passed from the man's memory. He was an art expert, and after a number of years he was invited to travel to an old Hall in Yorkshire to value the pictures. He saw the pictures; assessed them; then he asked the owner if there were any more. In an attic, he was told, there was a couple of paintings which had remained unhung for many years. The men went upstairs. There were two portraits, one of them of the cavalier whose head the art expert had previously seen in the Lyceum Theatre.

This was a great shock. The man made inquiries from the family, and learned that the portrait was one of an ancestor who had been beheaded in the early days of the Commonwealth. The family, perhaps collaterals of the Essex family, had owned the ground upon which the Lyceum Theatre had been built. It may be doubted if the woman in the theatre was ever conscious of the gruesome burden on her lap.

A much loved Victorian actor, William Terriss—the father of Ellaline Terriss and the father-in-law of the late Sir Seymour Hicks—who for long had been the idol of the public in melodramas at the Adelphi Theatre, was murdered by a mad actor, Richard Archer Prince, when he was playing the leading part in "Secret Service" on December 16th, 1897. Prince had gone to Terriss railing at some imaginary grievance of being slighted, and had received only kindness and the gift of golden sovereigns, with the advice that he go out and buy himself a good meal. For reward the "Mad Archer," wearing a black cloak and slouch hat, stabbed Terriss just as he was bending to put his key into the private door to the stage at the back of the Adelphi, in Maiden Lane.

Terriss staggered into the passage of the theatre, fell; and there, with his head supported by his leading lady, Jessie Milward, he died.

An example of premonition had preceded this most tragic event. A mummer called Lane, playing in the same company, on the night before the murder dreamt that he saw Bill Terriss lying bleeding on the steps inside the private door, while members of the company stood round him in amazed grief and horror, watching the beloved star die. Lane saw himself there too. He awoke filled with terror; but memory of his vision persisted and he felt constrained to tell other members of the cast about it. Although they laughed at him, treating the matter as a great joke, Lane unfortunately that evening saw his dream come true, with himself standing in exactly the same position as he had visualised in his dream.

The ghost of William Terriss was seen once in 1928. A man, who at the time had never heard of the murder, was walking in the narrow shadowy alley alongside the Adelphi Theatre. Suddenly he stared hard because he had seen a handsome old-fashioned figure pass him oddly dressed, with a flowing tie and a sombrero hat. The man was surprised and turned round to have another look, but the alley was empty and there had not been time for any living person to disappear. The man, who had never believed in ghosts, when told the facts of the murder, became convinced that he had seen the ghost of Terriss, particularly as the apparition must have vanished near the door through which the actor had so often entered the theatre, the last time to die.

But very recently in November, 1955, as reported in the *Sunday Dispatch* on January 15th, 1956, the ghost of William Terriss would appear to have been seen at Covent Garden Underground Station by several members of the station staff. A four-page report was sent to the London Transport Executive divisional headquarters concerning the statuesque figure of a man wearing a grey suit, old-fashioned collar and white gloves. . . . Foreman Collector Jack Hayden, one of those who saw this tall distinguished-looking spectre more than once, eventually rang headquarters at Leicester Square: "We have a ghost here," he said. Foreman Eric Davey, a spiritualist, was sent down and held a séance in the ante-room. Davey said: "I got the name Ter . . . something and a murder nearby. That evening somebody suggested Terriss." Pictures of the actor were found. They resembled a psychic sketch made by Davey. "That's him," Hayden said.

There are several stories of ghosts having been seen at the old Royalty Theatre in Dean Street, which was built in 1840 upon the site of a house that had stood there since the reign of Queen Anne. I have a special regard for the memory of the Royalty, with its gilded trappings, crushed strawberry curtains and carpets, tall fancy mirrors, and general over-decorated air of cosy intimate stuffiness, because it gave me my introduction to play-going. As might be expected there is report of a woman in a full white Queen Anne costume, who descends the staircase and fades out in the middle of the vestibule, some say with a shriek! A murdered woman's skeleton of that time was found in the basement, and her murderers, it is believed, were brought to justice. But in *Ghosts Over England* Mr. Thurston Hopkins gives a different version of this haunting. According to him "the spectre is a gypsy girl, dressed in a vivid green and scarlet silk gown and she rattles a tambourine as she wanders through the offices, which contain some of the rooms of the Queen Anne building. It is said that she makes her way down the stairs to the vestibule and vanishes. She only walks when the orchestra is playing, and it is the music of the violin (the devil's staff the gypsy calls it) which attracts her, for her lover was a Romany fiddler. She is always seeking to hear the magical fire of a gypsy violin. It is said that the Romany fiddler murdered the girl and buried her in a hollow wall of the ancient house which was afterwards incorporated in the Royalty Theatre. When the theatre was erected the workmen discovered the girl's almost mummified body in a tomb of plaster of Paris." And here there used to be still another ghost, a little old Victorian lady with ringlets, in a silk dress and bonnet, who was often to be observed trotting about the theatre with a cheerful smile, looking quite real. Like her brother phantom at Drury Lane, she is reputed to have been seen in the daytime by attendants and by playgoers alike, and to have mingled with the audience.

Of haunted provincial theatres some account of recent uncanny happenings at the Theatre Royal, Margate, may suffice as an example. The most curious psychic phenomenon reported from this old Georgian theatre, where the Victorian actress Sarah Thorne once ran a drama school, is a mysterious ball of light. The manifestation, it is alleged, is first seen in the auditorium, no bigger than a marble. The light travels over the footlights, across the stage, growing gradually larger until, by the time it disappears through the passage to the stage-door, it has become about the size of a football.

In late Georgian or early Victorian days, when there were stock companies, an actor in one of them who had been dismissed went to the box office of this theatre and bought himself a box for the next night's performance. During the course of the play he committed suicide by throwing himself out of his box into the orchestra-pit. Some time during the first decade of our century the wraith of a man appeared sitting motionless in the box, so often that the management was obliged to withdraw the box from sale, leaving it permanently curtained, until finally it was bricked up.

Has the ghost of this suicide, or of the actress Sarah Thorne, anything to do with new and startling phenomena which troubled this theatre as lately as the winter of 1955? We don't know. But in January of that year Mr. Howard Lee, the assistant stage manager, spoke of "the heavy front doors becoming unbolted twice in the early hours; of the foyer lights blazing on hours after they had been put out; and of a general feeling of eeriness." Mr. Lee's statement was supported by the caretaker, Mr. Robert Howell, who said: "Frequently when I've turned out the gas-lights backstage I have found them on again some time later. Often the sensation of uneasiness is almost overwhelming."

One day at their house in Venner Road, Sydenham, while I was enjoying conversation and tea with those two young, impressive theatrical archivists, Raymond Mander and Joe Mitchenson, Mr. Mitchenson told me how, on more than one occasion, he had been acutely conscious of the wraith of an old lady who had lived in his house from 1902 until 1910; the ghost had been seen also by his mother and by several other people between 1929 and 1949. Mr. Mitchenson had first the psychic impression that this discarnate old lady was mounting the stairs, then he saw her out of the tail of his eye just as she had reached the top of the stairs and was moving to turn into another room. Nothing more, but it sounded very convincing.

Mr. Mitchenson was also able to confirm the reality of the ghost at the Royalty Theatre in Dean Street. He was rehearsing in that theatre for a play called "Murder in Motley" in April, 1934. He was in the dress circle when he grew aware of an elderly lady seated quietly in the prompt box. "Am I seeing the famous Queen Anne lady?" he wondered. But when he went round to have a look, there was not a soul to be seen.

My final story deserts theatrical connexions, but for a ghost costumed in the uniform of a past epoch. The time was soon after midnight in September 1940, the scene 208, Old Brompton Road, the interior of a second-floor bedroom of a house built about 1860, converted into flats. Hitler had begun his blitz on London.

Mrs. Ruth Freeman, a Canadian artist friend of mine, had been sleeping lightly. She had woken up, for the air-raid siren had gone and she expected at any moment to be called out to her Warden's post. Her husband was already out on duty as a stretcher-bearer. She lay upon her side, staring nervously at the wall because her conviction was growing that there was somebody else in the room. She moved over and switched on the bedside lamp.

A man was sitting in the bedroom's large, comfortable armchair. He was wearing a navy-blue uniform, with epaulettes and a cockaded hat with a squarish peak that came low and hid his eyebrows, suggesting a soldier of the Napoleonic era. If the peaked cap hid the man's eyebrows it did not hide his eyes which, in a face that looked semi-transparent, were grey in colour and decent in their expression. It struck Mrs. Freeman that he seemed very sad. She felt that he was both sympathetic and embarrassed. It was as though he were trying to say to her: "Don't be afraid! I wish I wasn't here, but I can't help being here. I am more embarrassed to be here than you can possibly know." She was reassured, because she felt certain that, whoever he was, her visitor was a kind, nice person. The man remained, quiet and pensive in the arm-chair for perhaps twenty minutes, then he slowly faded away. Mrs. Freeman turned the light off and went to sleep.

For reasons unconnected with the apparition, the Freemans almost at once moved to another address. But three weeks after the ghost had been seen, that house was entirely demolished by a direct hit. Mrs. Freeman thought afterwards that the long cut of the phantom's head somewhat resembled in shape the head of her brother. Could the ghost, she wonders, with its sad expression, have been the spirit of an ancestor come to warn her of impending, imminent disaster?

Chapter Eleven

Haunted Pubs, and the Runcorn Poltergeist

UNTIL I began to write upon the subject of ghosts, I had not realised that alleged stories of hauntings were so numerous; that supposed psychic entities in one form or another, even supernormal appearances, were apparently almost two a penny. Once people find out that your own interest in such matters is serious, they are ready to tell you their personal experiences, I believe nearly always with complete sincerity. There is less motive for dishonesty in the domain of ghosts than there is, for example, in the province of mediumship, where planned fraud may sometimes more easily be equated with cash gains! But although tales accumulate, adding up to more than enough material for several books, caution is needed; every claim must be judged and tested, so far as possible, upon its own merits because fallible human beings, though of the utmost good faith, may none the less be self-deceived. Meanwhile, it should be an aim of the official science of the future to explore these mysteries for us.

Out of the innumerable public houses that exist in England, I have had some personal contact with three which are said to be haunted, in Somerset, in Sussex, and in London. A few miles outside Taunton, at Culmhead up in the Blackdown Hills, there is a small stone whitewashed country inn, "The Holman Clavel," kept for the last seven years by Mr. and Mrs. Leslie Phillips, an ordinary sensible middle-aged couple, who talked to me about their poltergeist in such a sober manner that I could not doubt they believed in it. The inn, dating back some six hundred years, was once a farm bailiff's cottage, when the land belonged to the Church. Today it is low-ceilinged, with black beams, and has a skittle-alley at the back. The previous landlord warned Mrs. Phillips's mother, when they moved in, that "the bloody place is haunted!"

But "Charlie," their poltergeist, is more mischievous than frightening. He plays skittles, walks about at night, sometimes produces loud crashes, and occasionally appropriates articles, such as a key, a 10s. postal order win from Littlewoods, a sheet of insurance stamps, which, however, he returns after intervals of months. On entering the bar one morning Mr. Phillips found that a seven-pint enamel jug was full to the brim with beer, although he was positive it had been empty when the household went to bed on the previous night. Another trick of "Charlie" was to take and five weeks later restore a missing tablecloth, which was found in the drawer where it was habitually kept, freshly laundered, lying neat in clean undisturbed folds.

Here it was the Skittles at Midnight that interested me most, with "Charlie's" apparent fondness for this popular long-alley game. I visited the skittle-alley and know that the balls make a considerable noise. There is a bungalow close to the inn, which Mr. Phillips lets in summer. Two separate parties of visitors, one from Wales, the other from London, who stayed in it during the first weeks of August in 1952 and 1953 declared they heard the skittle-alley in use in the early hours of the morning long after the landlord and his wife were in bed, both inn and skittle-alley being securely locked up. "They're on the late skittles tonight!" Culmhead people have said. "We heard the pins and balls."

The imagination is fired by the thought of the sound of those large wooden balls, impelled by a ghostly hand, rolling down the alley at dead of night, and the pins scattering.

Although Mr. and Mrs. Phillips refused to allow a séance to be held at "The Holman Clavel," they admit to having heard noises which have made them sit up in bed at night—one sounding as if a shelf in the bar had crashed to the ground. I spoke also to their son, Howard, who told me that some while ago, when serving in the Colonial Police, he came home from abroad, and late one night he went to the bathroom. Suddenly he heard padding footsteps, coming nearer from the landing. The bathroom door-handle turned, the sound of footsteps entered, moved round, went out again. The door closed, the footsteps padded away along the landing. The boy, who was then in his late teens, furthermore had sensed a presence. He was shocked and shaken. He said: "Well, Dad, if there is such a thing as ghosts, I've heard one now."

"The King's Arms" at Rotherfield, near Crowborough in Sussex, is, or was until very recently, haunted. This ancient hostelry is believed to have once been a tithe barn where corn was bought and sold, and there is a legend of a miller who is supposed to have hanged himself. Be that as it may, in 1953 the landlord was Maurice Tate, former Sussex and England cricketer, and after what happened he and his family are strongly inclined to believe that ghosts exist. This is a ghost that is never seen, but has been heard upon the evening of the same date for succeeding years, late in June. As Mrs. Kay Tate put it: "It was about eight o'clock on that Saturday evening. I was in the bar with my son and daughter, Betty, and my daughter-in-law. Mr. Tate was out. All at once we heard heavy footsteps running like mad up the stairs and along the corridor above the bar—which corridor is a dead end, only bedrooms lead out of it. Well, you see we feared thieves and went upstairs immediately to look. There was nobody there. And exactly the same thing had happened just a year before."

One night Maurice Tate went upstairs to fetch some change from a bedroom his family called the "special" room. He felt somebody touch him so plainly that he turned round and asked: "What do you want?" thinking it was one of his children. The room was empty. His daughter had once similarly felt somebody touch her in the same room, when there was nobody to be seen.

And then in 1954 on the same date in June the present licensee, Mr. Hilary Ball, noted that at precisely 7.40 p.m. he heard what he describes as "light, hurried footsteps in the passage overhead," while he was serving in the bar. His daughter, Jill Ball, an attractive and intelligent member of the young generation who is training to be a doctor, added her corroborative evidence that she, too, had heard the footsteps on another occasion and was quite persuaded of the reality of the ghost. Mrs. Ball had heard the ghost also, and told me that in December 1954, when she was upstairs in the passage between 5 p.m. and 6 p.m. sorting clothes from a cupboard, she saw, glancing sideways, what looked like a young girl's naked feet. On the anniversary in June, 1955, unfortunately, the ghost failed to make its presence known.

Visitors to that fashionable London pub, "The Grenadier," 18, Wilton Row, may read something of its history and its ghost for themselves in the bar where a few facts hang framed, which read as follows: "Set in a quiet mews with the sound of traffic circling Hyde Park Corner lies the *Grenadier*—it was once an inn that served as a mess for the officers of regiments stationed near by. The military association can be clearly recognised when you read the name of the alley which runs beside the pub—Old Barrack Yard—for it was on this ground that the soldiers of yesterday drilled and manoeuvred.

"In those days the public drank in what is now called the cellar. The present bar served as a dining-room for the military officers. As with many old buildings the place has its ghost. During the month of September—and the landlord's wife can vouch for this—there walks the spirit of a grenadier who is reputed to have been flogged to death in the room which is now the bar." He is supposed to have been caught cheating at cards and too rough justice was administered.

"The grand old Duke of Wellington is said to have known the place well and to have used it frequently. His horses were stabled near by and a mounting block he would have used stands in the mews near by outside."

Although Mr. Roy Grigg, the present licensee, is a little doubtful of the grenadier story, he is certain that his inn is haunted. He asserts that the house takes on sometimes a peculiar menacing atmosphere, and that it could provide, over the last forty years or so, a history of unfortunate events in the domestic lives of those who have lived on the premises. Often, he says, after the bar closes at night the place turns cold and upstairs feels somehow unwelcome, so that he is inclined to put off going to bed. The psychic tension would appear to build up through the year, reaching its climax in September. During the first fortnight of that month his young Alsatian dog always reacts strongly, showing every sign of terrified unrest, growling, snarling, with hackles raised, and sometimes trying to scratch and dig in the cellar. Both a barman and a cleaner have watched, and confirm, this behaviour of the dog.

In September or October, 1952, Mr. Grigg's son, who was then nine years old, was lying in bed with his door open. The boy complained of the shadow of a person reflected upon his bedroom wall from the landing, where the light was on—growing larger, then smaller, advancing and retreating, like someone hesitating to come in. The same year Mr. Grigg's wife was changing in her bedroom upstairs at noon. Believing herself to be alone at the top of the house, she had left her door wide open and was indignant, as she was half undressed, to see a man's figure coming up the stairs. But it was nobody human who could be accounted for, and the figure vanished. The following year Mrs. Ward, the proprietress of "The Three Jolly Gardeners" in Hammersmith, was drinking in the bar of "The Grenadier" when she distinctly saw a man going upstairs, who proved to have no objective reality.

Lastly, in 1953, a Roman Catholic boyhood friend of Roy Grigg had driven Mr. Grigg's family up from Plymouth, and stayed the night at "The Grenadier" in a bedroom about which he had heard disturbing warnings from a Roman Catholic barman. So he hung his rosary over the bed in order to ensure a good night's rest. He did not get it. He felt somebody standing by his bed trying to touch him, and there was a sharp drop in temperature. It would seem that there is something here for the psychic researcher.

I come now to what, so far as I know, is the most well attested, and in one part the most sinister, recent story of poltergeist phenomena in England, the fantastic "hauntings" at Runcorn, Cheshire. The sequence of events is not a simple one, and it is difficult to make any one theory fit in with the facts; but these odd happenings were carefully investigated by several intelligent, experienced, and reliable witnesses, so that upon the evidence I have studied I believe the case to be genuine. If at the end of my account the reader should feel only extreme bewilderment and be silently protesting "but in everyday life these things cannot happen!" I would agree that the events on the farm are not easily believable. And yet to the open-minded inquirer proved "paranormal occurrences compel revision of concepts" and "facts are more stubborn than beliefs." I am deeply grateful for the generous help given to me by the Rev. W. H. Stevens, Superintendent Methodist Minister in Widnes, by means of letters and a dossier on the case. Mr. Stevens, who was later appointed as official investigator by the S.P.R., in one of his letters to me writes:

"My connection with the Runcorn 'Haunting' arose from the fact that, being a Methodist Minister, I was stationed in Widnes which is just across the Mersey from Runcorn. Reading about it in the Press I went over to investigate in a sceptical frame of mind. For about thirty years I have been a member of the London S.P.R., have read scores of books on the subject, attended various séances, had sittings with mediums—all in my search for truth. Consequently, I knew what to expect on the general behaviour of poltergeists. Gradually I came to the conclusion that this was a genuine case. The most unexpected and unorthodox occurrences were those on the farm. Knowing the Crowthers and having been to the farm I cannot doubt their story. They had been badly frightened and upset. It is impossible but true."

"The boy complained of the shadow of a person reflected upon his bedroom wall . . . advancing and retreating, like someone hesitating to come in."

The strange happenings at No. 1 Byron Street, Runcorn, began on Sunday, August 17th, 1952. At the outset it may be worth mentioning, as possibly of some significance, that (as with my friends the Colliers's poltergeist at Prestbury) over the ensuing weeks the most violent phenomena and manifestations of malevolence occurred on Sundays. The house, built sixty-five years previously, was an ordinary working-class cottage standing at the corner of a row which extends into the next street. At the time the household consisted of the following members: Mr. Sam Jones, in his late sixties, a widower who had occupied the house for the past thirty-three years; Mrs. Lucy Jones, a widow, the daughter-in-law of Mr. Jones; the grandson John Glynn, aged seventeen, around whom the phenomena centred; Miss Ellen Whittle, a forty-nine-year-old lodger; and a child aged eight who slept elsewhere during the disturbances.

The bedroom, to which the manifestations were confined, was a small, sparsely furnished room which had two additional doors, one leading into an empty clothes closet, the other down three steps to a bedroom occupied by Miss Whittle. In the middle of the room was a heavy, iron double bedstead, and a single bed stood against the wall opposite the window. Near the window was the dressing-table, and between the two beds stood a large empty chest weighing about 50 lb. The trouble started that Sunday night with Mr. Sam Jones and John Glynn who shared the room, after they had gone to bed and put the light out, hearing what sounded like scratching in a drawer of the dressing-table. They could find no mouse, nor anything to account for this, and the scratching was renewed, to be succeeded on other nights by far more violent sounds, loud knockings hammered the silence—a clock smashed itself against the wall, books were hurled by invisible hands, the dressing-table rocked giddily. Suspecting a practical joker, Mr. Jones reported the matter to the police; but when the police could find nothing normal to account for the trouble, they officially withdrew. Before this unearthly haunting faded out, it had been investigated by as many as thirty independent witnesses, including a team of three sent up by the B.B.C. under the producer Mr. Dennis Mitchell, which, however, drew almost negative results. This was not until October and they may have been too late. But the case caused a great deal of excitement in Runcorn, and crowds of people gathered outside the house. The noise of the disturbances could be heard in the street.

Before I select from the full account of his investigation sent to me by Mr. W. H. Stevens, and quote also from the evidence of other witnesses, it may be said that in the opinion of those who knew him John Glynn appeared to be a normal boy of average intelligence, bright, pleasant and of a kindly nature, with the carefree spirit of youth. He seemed neither unbalanced nor neurotic; but naturally he was not unaffected by four months of poltergeist persecution, though he was no nervous wreck. Of John Glynn's friend Mr. Stevens writes: "Johnny Berry was of a placid disposition and took everything in his stride. Though at times he showed signs of fear, yet nothing seemed to revolve around him personally. The kingpin was John Glynn." John Glynn had persuaded his eighteen-year-old friend to sleep with him for company. Of his own investigation Mr. Stevens reports:

"On the first night of my visit, after the lights had been switched off and all was quiet, the dressing-table suddenly began to creak loudly and was dragged across the floor. Light was switched on, but there appeared to have been no movement on the part of anyone in the room. It was a medium-sized dressing-table, with the drawers full of clothes, etc. I pushed it back again. Soon after, amid loud creaking, it was dragged along the floor and began to shake violently. Addressing the table, I said: 'If you can hear my voice, knock three times.' Immediately it shook vigorously once, twice, and at the third shake I shone my torch at the same time as a friend of mine, Mr. J. C. Davies, switched on the light. There was the dressing-table shaking and rattling with no one near. The two youths were wrapped up in the bedclothes. I went over to see whether the table would shake if given a start, but it was quite firm on the floor. Endeavours to establish a code of communication met with no result."

Mr. Davies, an independent and reliable witness, having no connexion with the families concerned, writes in support of Mr. Stevens's account: "To my great astonishment the dresser continued in full light to beat itself against the wall, rocking *violently*. This, I imagine, continued for about three seconds, and certainly there was no possibility of physical contact from the bed. I lay on the bed and attempted to move the dresser from a lying position with my hand. Although with an effort I could do this, I was quite unable to simulate the previous movement, which had been extremely rapid."

Mr. Stevens, Mr. Davies, Mr. Harold Crowther, and other witnesses, all agree that various objects were sent flying across the bedroom; also that there was certainly no preliminary sound of movement from the bed itself. Some objects, torches, an alarm clock, books, crashed against the walls, sometimes penetrating the plaster to the brickwork and leaving scars. A book—a dictionary—once hit Mr. Stevens gently on the head. The pillows were sent across the room from under the heads of the boys and John Glynn appeared to be flung out of bed. The boys claimed that several times they had felt themselves pulled by a force they could not resist.

At first Mr. Stevens had regarded the boys with a certain amount of natural scepticism and suspicion; for things can be deliberately thrown under cover of darkness. But though he used his torch frequently, he failed to detect any trickery. "Had the boys got out of bed or even sat up," he says, "the movement of the clothes and certainly the creaking of the bed (and it did creak) would have been heard. Besides, we were very close to them, and sometimes I would kneel down and place my arm lightly across the bedclothes in the dark ready to detect any possible movement. When the B.B.C. van visited the house the boys were very anxious that something should happen. An unsteady table had been rigged up from the remains of the by-then-smashed dressing-table, and a few articles had been placed on top as tempting ammunition. With me there were two other people in the room and we stood a distance away. The boys knew where we were and conditions were ideal for fraud. It would have been the easiest thing in the world for Johnny Berry to reach out his hand in the dark and throw things from the table or knock the whole contraption over, but nothing happened.

"John Glynn would never lie on the side of the bed next to the dressing-table. There was genuine fear among the family; and though the boys became used to the excitement of the disturbances, yet they showed nervousness when left alone with just one or two of us. They would not remain in the room without someone being present.

"On one occasion I pulled the dressing-table to the foot of the bed, pushing it against the wall out of reach of the youths. Replacing various articles, I put a box containing a jig-saw puzzle behind two books close to where I stood. No one else was in that part of the room and there was dead silence. My torch was at the ready. One after the other the things on the dressing-table were sent across the room. I could hear the two books leaving the table, then the rattle of the jig-saw in the box. Immediately I shone my torch, while at the same time Mr. Davies switched on the light with its 100-watt bulb. The jig-saw was travelling across the room about seven feet in the air. The two boys were lying with the bed-clothes pulled around them; no creak of the bed or rustle of the clothes had been heard." Mr. Davies, confirming this incident, has written: "I distinctly saw in excellent light a cardboard box almost in suspension above the bed. The behaviour of this box was not that of an ordinary trajectory, but almost as if it were being carried with directional intent." Of another time he writes: "I visited the house on my way to business one morning about 10 o'clock and was met at the door by Mrs. Lucy Jones who was in a state of great anxiety and was obviously ill with the strain. I was shown the bedroom and the stairs. It appears that the previous night all the furniture in the bedroom had been overturned and pillows ripped up and feathers were very much in evidence both on the stairs and in the bedroom."

A third investigator Mr. Harold Crowther, a farmer in Runcorn who was anxious to find a solution to the mystery, after his own horrible experiences upon his farm which follow, told Mr. Stevens that once he put his overcoat on the dressing-table, remarking, "If you don't want it, give it back to me,' and that the coat was thrown back to him three times in succession. The next night, after things had been thrown about the room, he suggested, "Why not put them back for a change?" He heard a movement, flashed on his torch and declared he actually saw the drawer moving across the bed towards the dressing-table!

At times the large chest between the two beds would bang on the floor, and once it struck the single bed with such force that the bed was moved about four inches when four people were sitting on it. Mr. Crowther sat on the chest after it had been moving. He said that he felt it vibrate under him. As for the dressing-table, it was pulled to pieces during the disturbances which would have required a feat of strength beyond any normal unpremeditated human action.

Before I describe Mr. Crowther's worst experiences, it may be worth noting that a tragedy came to No. 1 Byron Street on the night of October 22nd, although there is no evidence to connect this easily with the poltergeist. Miss Ellen Whittle, who for the past fifteen years had occupied the room adjoining the bedroom where the activity occurred, was out for an evening walk and fell forty feet into a disused old sandstone quarry known as the Frog's Mouth. She died from shock and multiple injuries in hospital the next day.

When the Rev. W. H. Stevens heard that Mr. and Mrs. Crowther had had distressing experiences at their fifteenth-century farmhouse home, Runcorn, which seemed to be linked with the poltergeist haunting at Byron Street, he called to see them on July 31st, 1953. Mr. Sam Jones was a part-time worker on the farm, having been employed there a few months before the outbreaks in Byron Street. It could be that the poltergeist started on the farm and later attached itself to John Glynn. The Crowthers, well-known and respected people, had shunned Press publicity; but their story was told in the *Sunday Graphic*, December 27th, 1953, and in the *Liverpool Echo*, August 28th, 1954, so it is now part of humanity's store of uncommon knowledge. It is a story, I should imagine, without parallel—that of the deaths of all Mr. Crowther's pedigree pigs, fifty-three in number, by a supernatural agent. Signed statements by Mr. and Mrs. Crowther as to its veracity were sent by Mr. Stevens with a Report to the S.P.R.

It all began when Mrs. Crowther was making a long-distance call on the farm telephone. While waiting, she saw Mr. Crowther's deceased father standing a few yards away. He was dressed as usual, was wearing spectacles, and was smoking a cigarette with a long ash, which was characteristic of him. Mrs. Crowther stared in amazement, and when her call came through, she has said: "I hardly knew what I was saying, for I could still see him, then he vanished." After the last pig had died she saw the apparition again outside, while she was cleaning, in one of the sties. Mr. Stevens comments: "The Crowthers are well respected people. They told me their story with obvious sincerity, and it was plain to see they had passed through a distressing period. Mr. Crowther was in bed for a fortnight with a breakdown. They had no knowledge of, nor interest in, Spiritualism."

On Monday, August 11th, 1952, a week before the Byron Street disturbances began, the first pig died. They attached no significance to it. Before the end of the week several more pigs had died, and by the end of a fortnight they had lost all fifty-three. Five veterinary surgeons had been called in to examine the bodies; entrails were sent away for analysis; but the cause of these mysterious deaths remained a mystery.

Two days after the loss of his last pig, Mr. Crowther was astonished to see what he described as "a large black cloud about seven feet in height, shapeless except for two prongs sticking out at the back," moving about in the yard. The shapeless mass approached him, stopping about four or five feet away. When he went nearer, it moved round to his left side, turned in the direction of the pig sties, passed into an outhouse and disappeared. Mr. Crowther mentioned this curious experience to no one, afraid of being thought "queer"; but, three days later, his wife told him that she had seen a strange dark cloud floating about the yard. "Don't tell me you've seen it too!" Mr. Crowther exclaimed. Whether the pigs saw anything or not, the fact is that something frightened them. Some fought. In one sty a terrified animal was found trying to climb up the wall as if to escape.

One night a cow's bellowings were heard, unusually loud and

prolonged. The animal was discovered in a state of intense fear, its eyes bulging, the hair on its back on end, its body covered with beads of sweat. No cause for alarm could be diagnosed, but from that night the cow gave no more milk.

Now scratchings were occasionally heard coming from the drawers of a desk in the farm kitchen. Then the drawers would rattle violently, jam-pots on the shelves would be overturned—typical poltergeist manifestations. Mr. Sam Jones was soon telling Mr. Crowther about the disquieting disturbances in his house in Byron Street, and was so stricken from lack of sleep and frayed nerves that he broke down and sobbed. He implored Mr. Crowther to come and help him to investigate, and Mr. Crowther was ultimately persuaded. Mr. Crowther's first visit coincided with that of Mr. Stevens, who says that, while there, on two occasions Mr. Crowther declares he saw the same black cloud with its two prongs on the bed where the boys were lying. He caught sight of it in the light of his torch; then it faded away.

The end of the cloud was this. On December 6th, just after the alarming upheavals in Byron Street had ceased, Mr. Crowther saw it at twilight in his farm kitchen. Determined to find out what it was, he made for the light switch, and as he brushed past the cloud, the two prongs touched him on the left side of his throat. They felt solid, like two blunt sticks. As soon as he switched on the light the cloud had disappeared.

It made one more, final appearance. On the morning of December 13th, 1952, Mr. Crowther opened the door of a large shed in which he kept two dogs, a spaniel and a sheep dog. On finding themselves released, the dogs rushed out excitedly. Turning round, Mr. Crowther saw the cloud on his left side, smaller and lighter-looking. It moved along the ground, rose up in the air and disintegrated. The dogs must have seen it too, for they were barking and jumping up towards it.

That was the last of the cloud. Mr. Crowther had suffered serious financial loss. The pig farm has now become a mushroom farm. Never again, says Mr. Crowther, dare he keep another pig.

Mrs. Crowther's evidence supports that of her husband. She was a witness to the loud rattling of the drawers and the turning over of the jam-pots in the farm kitchen. She saw the cloud in the yard. It blotted out the houses in the background. As it moved along bits of paper and dust swirled about as though they were caught up by a miniature whirlwind.

In a letter dated August 31st, 1953, addressed to the Rev. W. H. Stevens, Mrs. Crowther has written: "I saw the cloud twice, once in the yard when it was huge, and once in the kitchen when Mr. Jones called on Armistice Sunday. I saw the thing follow Mr. Jones. It was much smaller and more sprawled out. At no time did I see the prongs. It just travelled like smoke when drawn by suction."

Such strange matters are at present beyond the reach and proof of science, and may long remain so. Most men are too materialistic to consider a conception of life's meaning in terms beyond the world of their five normal senses, and tend unwisely to reject anything that is foreign to their habitual scene of common experience. Perhaps, as Mr. Stevens wisely suggests, "our picture is not big enough, it is too simple, too materialistic. . . . The world as presented to our senses and the world of reality will have many differences."

Chapter Twelve

Photographs of Ghosts and Conclusion

AN excellent book first published in 1956, *The Unknown, Is It Nearer?* by E. J. Dingwall and John Langdon-Davies, concludes with the authors' answer to the title: "Yes, the Unknown is nearer and is likely to be much nearer still in the not very distant future." Anybody who is interested in alleged supernatural experiences or in the strict analysis of supposed paranormal phenomena should find this book fascinating and, within its terms, convincing because of the authors' scientific method and judicial approach to their subject matter. In a chapter entitled "Apparitions And Haunted Houses" are set out ten points for testing the likelihood of a ghost story proving true, the last point enumerated being this: "You cannot photograph a real ghost, nor record its sounds on a recording machine." I have neither the wish nor the qualifications to contradict Dr. Dingwall, who is among the most experienced members of the S.P.R., and I note the distinction "a real ghost." All I claim with regard to the first part of this statement, in view of the incidents which follow, is a layman's right to question; to wonder whether the expert need necessarily always be correct?

It is now well known that the S.P.R. have recently published in *The Haunting of Borley Rectory* a painstaking and, for the most part damaging, report by three of their experts, including Dr. Dingwall, on the evidence for the genuineness of the very numerous paranormal happenings at the "Most Haunted House in England." Though they conclude that one or two of the incidents at Borley seem inexplicable, the report contains charges of trickery against Harry Price and against Mrs. Foyster, the young wife of an elderly incumbent since dead. "The inquiry," said *The Times*, reviewing the book, "seems to have begun after Price's death in 1948. His files have been used, but his personal testimony might have been relevant, as might that of the young wife concerned." I have touched on this matter because, in spite of the many grounds for scepticism unearthed by the S.P.R., there are those who maintain that since the Rectory was burnt down in 1939 the hauntings have gone on, and because of a photograph taken by Mr. Godfrey Thurston Hopkins of the gatepost—about all that is left—in 1955.

Mr. R. Thurston Hopkins, while kindly entertaining me at Brighton, told me that his son, Godfrey, a distinguished photographer of long standing on *Picture Post* who has photographed all over the world, taking an average of about a thousand photographs a week, had never previously had any unorthodox blur or speck on his negatives. He went to Borley in a sceptical frame of mind to shoot the surviving relics and took, almost idly, a picture of the gatepost, behind which ran a fence of palings and wire. It was mid-afternoon, with a clear sky. Mr. Thurston Hopkins "wanted sharply to outline the gatepost and fence against the sky" and has stated most definitely that the resultant dark mass did not appear in the viewfinder and that he cannot explain it. Did the film in his camera perhaps record the famous Borley nun, who was supposed to have been strangled there in the seventeenth century? For people claim to have seen the ghost of the nun as "a dark shadow." This remarkable photograph has been widely reproduced in various papers, which include

Picture Post, January 1st, 1955 and *Photoguide Magazine*, January, 1956. All Mr. Hopkins's work is developed and printed in the darkroom at the *Picture Post* office, London. Another staff photographer, Mr. Alex Dellow, was sent to Borley to try and corroborate the first camera's evidence. His picture of the same scene taken from exactly the same angle was completely clear, and he was emphatic that the photographed "ghost" could not have been caused by any "intruding bough or by any other natural image or mirage."

Mrs. Dyer, the Reading baby-farmer, did more than come back to haunt Chief Warder Scott at Newgate. Mr. R. Thurston Hopkins has told how "just before the prison was closed a press photographer came to take pictures of Newgate and some of the officials. He snapped Chief Warder Scott and Doctor Scott (afterwards Governor of Holloway Prison) standing outside the execution shed. They had been talking about old days, and had reminisced about Mrs. Dyer."

Apparently, Doctor Scott was an amateur photographer, who had fitted up a darkroom in the prison. The press photographer took the opportunity of developing one or two of his plates to make certain they were "pin-sharp," knowing that this was the last time it would be possible to photograph Newgate. He came out of the darkroom, bewilderedly muttering: "It just beats me, there's a woman's face looking over Mr. Scott's shoulder. 'Tisn't possible!"

There was a woman's face, and Chief Warder Scott was sure that it was Mrs. Dyer. It is only fair to add that the photographer, to justify his incredulity, suggested that it might have been Doctor Scott's hand resting on the warder's shoulder, which moved and produced the blurred outline of a face.

What are we to make of such instances? I know little technical about photography; yet I know that the use of infra-red light will enable the camera eye to detect, for example, underlying figures in a forged cheque invisible to the human eye. We think of the camera as a "mere machine"; but could it be possible for the film in a camera to catch a ghost where something in the human eye inhibits the sight of an apparition? Could a machine behave as a psychic sensitive or medium, responsive to some past impression indelibly recorded upon the ether? From a number of records it would seem that this might not be an altogether fantastic explanation, particularly when we remember how little is known about the ether. In Webster's Dictionary occurs this definition of the ether in Physics: "A hypothetical medium supposed to fill all known space, even those portions occupied by fluids and solids. The functions assigned to the ether, such as the transmission of transverse waves with the velocity of light and the production, when under certain strains or subjected to certain motions, of all the phenomena due to electric and magnetic fields of force, indicate properties unlike those of any known form of matter. The difficulty of forming any accurate conception of the nature and structure of the ether is very great, and the prevailing views concerning it are, as yet, speculative."

My brother-in-law, Stuart Legg, whose name is a distinguished one in the world of documentary films, sends me an interesting account of an apparent ghost-photograph taken in Canada. At the time he was Chief Producer to the National Film Board of Canada. Though the crew of two who went North were not actually working for him, they showed him the photograph in question as a curiosity and he recalls it well. Stuart Legg writes:

"In Canada, there is a legend concerning one of the trading-posts of the Hudson's Bay Company. These posts, which are scattered across the immensities of the Arctic north, are traditionally in charge of a 'factor,' who is often alone, and whose duty is to buy furs brought in by the Indian or Esquimo trappers.

"The story runs that during the eighteenth century one of the more isolated of the Company's posts was managed by a factor of morose and evil-tempered disposition. It happened that about the time of the onset of winter, a traveller arrived at the post and asked for shelter during the winter months. In such country an emergency request of this kind was—and is—never refused. The factor, however, declined point blank to take the traveller in, indicating that so far as he was concerned, he could go to the devil. To turn a man away into the white wastes of the northern winter, with its ferocious blizzards and dangerous sub-zero temperatures, is, of course, tantamount to murder; and the factor must have been perfectly aware of this. But he persisted in his refusal. A quarrel developed; blows were struck; and one of the men was killed.

"Canada was a tough country in those days. A case of murder was nothing extraordinary, and no doubt the tale would never have been resurrected but for an odd episode which took place about fifteen years ago. During the late war, the National Film Board in Ottawa had occasion to send a film crew of two men into the North. On their journey they happened to stop off at the same Hudson's Bay post—though they knew nothing of the story connected with it. The morning after their arrival a sled was being loaded outside the main building of the post, and they took a still photograph of the proceedings. They noticed nothing peculiar at the time; and the picture was duly returned to Ottawa, along with their other exposed negatives, for processing. On being developed and printed, the photograph showed a typical scene of the kind: on the right, the building of the post; at centre, the factor and his assistants busy with crates and cords about the sled; to the left, the harnessed dogs sitting waiting in the snow, and behind them a belt of the pine trees characteristic of the country. A peculiarity, however, now became apparent. Near the left-hand edge of the picture, and close to the leading dogs, was a human figure. It was less dense than the figures of the other men present, and appeared somewhat blurred; but was of approximately the same size. It was difficult, owing to the lightness and blurring, to identify the clothes except for one feature: the headgear. The figure had on its head a tam o'shanter: a broad, flat crown surmounted by the usual woolly ball; and beneath the crown, a chequered tartan band encircling the head. Such a tam o'shanter must be almost unknown in Canada today—save possibly at big ice-hockey or baseball games. It would certainly be a matter of amused remark in the North, where either fur caps, leather helmets, or long-visored American caps are the standard head-dress.

"The two cameramen who shot the picture expressed themselves as certain on the following points: (1) They themselves were both behind the camera when they took the photograph, and everyone else at the post at the time was helping to load the sled and was accounted for in the picture; (2) No one had been standing near the leading dogs; (3) It would have been unlikely to the point of absurdity for a stranger, in that empty land, suddenly to turn up out of the blue and pose himself in the picture; (4) They had not seen a tam o'shanter of the kind revealed in the picture—or of any kind—since their arrival, and were sure that they would have recalled it if they had.

"The photograph, with a description of the circumstances, was sent to the headquarters of the Hudson's Bay Company in Winnipeg, with a request for any light they could shed. In reply, the Company indicated the existence of the long-dead legend outlined above. They also commented that while a tam o'shanter such as the figure was wearing would be a rarity today, it was a common head-dress in former centuries, since a large proportion of the personnel stationed at the posts were—as they still are—of Scottish origin."

In *The Imprisoned Splendour*, An approach to Reality, based upon the significance of data drawn from the fields of Natural Science, Psychical Research and Mystical Experience (commended to the public in a Foreword by the Rev. Leslie D. Weatherhead "with immense enthusiasm and without reserve" as "this enthralling and stimulating book"), the author Raynor C. Johnson, M.A. (Oxon), Ph.D., D.Sc. (Lond.) Master of Queen's College, University of Melbourne, makes his position plain with regard to the possibility of photographing ghosts. Briefly, his theory is that ghosts are physical. "I would maintain," he writes, "that they *do* reflect in a limited degree ordinary light-waves. Because of their transience and unheralded appearance, the possibilities of photography are obviously quite small, but there is one noteworthy instance where a photograph was obtained...."

He goes on to tell of the famous ghost-photograph taken at Raynham Hall, Norfolk, seat of the Marquess of Townshend, which was published more than once, for example in *Coming Events in Britain*, December 1951. The photograph is well known. It is Mr. Raynor Johnson's theory that is of such enormous interest:

"Expressed in the simplest terms," he says, "I regard the telepathic thought-form as the animating principle or transient 'mind' which clothes itself in an aetheric body. This may condense enough chemical matter around it to reflect light. The extent to which it does this seems to differ greatly: sometimes the figure is transparent and the background can be seen through it; at other times it has a solidity indistinguishable from an ordinary figure."

The Rev. W. H. Stevens, who assumed such a prominent part in the Runcorn haunting, after referring in a letter to the incident of the Raynham Hall ghost-photograph, has told me: "A similar incident took place in Dora's Field at Rydal near here, in 1951. A visitor took a photograph of the field when the daffodils were in full bloom. On the film there appeared two ladies apparently in conversation, one was a nun, the other a lady in Elizabethan dress. The figures are clear and natural. No one was in sight during the taking of the picture. A party of overseas visitors witnessed to the fact."

I have beside me on my desk as I write, a mahogany framed photograph which is a mounted enlargement of a snapshot taken nearly fifty years ago. Although no conventional ghost appears in it, I believe this photograph to include the genuine "psychic" portrait of a little girl. It is a most treasured possession—generously lent to me, for there is none other—of an old friend, Mrs. Elizabeth Priestley, of Newhouse Farm, Tidebrook, near Wadhurst, and is of her late father-in-law, Seacome Ellison Priestley. The curious story of the photograph is this:

About the year 1912 Mr. Priestley was on holiday at Shap in Westmorland with his wife and daughter, Dorothy, who was then in her twenties. One afternoon father and daughter were walking along a lonely road which ran across the moors. The road was long and quite deserted; not a soul was in sight, not a child, not a dog, not a rabbit. The daughter said that she would like to take a photograph of her father with her "box Brownie" camera, which she proceeded to do, he standing in tweed cap and mackintosh blown forward by the wind at the side of the road, his stick under his arm, holding his field-glasses. When the negative was developed and printed, the photograph clearly showed, beyond Mr. Priestley, looking over a tuft of grass in the ditch on the far side of the road, a little girl of about five or six years old. The child appeared much less than life-size, with a pretty mischievous face, a woolly cap tilted back on her head showing her curls, one hand to her mouth. And it was the daughter, Dorothy Priestley, just as she had looked when a child of that age!

The photograph was examined by both Sir Oliver Lodge and by Sir Arthur Conan Doyle, who each declared it to be a spirit photograph, possibly born out of the father's thoughts while he was being taken. There are no grounds at all for suspecting fraud.

I possess a beautiful colour print of two ghostly figures on the steps going up to the Chapter House in Wells Cathedral, Somerset. Such a rarity came to me in a manner that seemed like the working of Providence. From Farnham I telephoned a friend, H. R. Hardy of Edgeborough, Frensham, whom I had not seen for several years, and he asked me what I was doing. I replied that I was writing a book about ghosts; then lightly inquired if he knew anything about them. "No," he answered, "but I've got a coloured photograph of one! If you care to come over, I will throw it on the screen for you." At once, I was into my car and away. I saw the enlargement on the screen, was allowed to borrow the negative, and so obtained my print. There are two figures—a small child and a much taller, perhaps maternal figure in white—standing framed in the archway at the entrance to the covered archway leading over the road to Vicars' Close. Here is Mr. Hardy's first-hand account of how the photograph was taken:

"The facts are that I went to Wells on Easter Monday, April 19th, 1954, in the afternoon. I should think the photo was taken about 4.30 p.m. Seeing that there were a lot of people going around, I thought I should fail to get an uninterrupted exposure of the steps going up to the Chapter House. However, I set up my stand, and, seeing a lull, pressed the shutter and gave it an exposure of 14 seconds, watching *very* carefully to see that

"... the photograph clearly showed, looking over a tuft of grass on the far side of the road, a little girl of about five or six years old."

no one should walk in to spoil the photo. I counted fourteen, and did not look at my wrist-watch as I was afraid I should then not see if anyone did walk into the picture. I heaved a sigh of relief when nobody did.

"The 'fluffiness' on the steps may have been caused by light coming in from a window out of sight on the left, though it does not really look like that. It reminds me much more of heads going up or down the steps. I can give no explanation of the two figures framed in the archway. I might just emphasise that if the cluster on the staircase was not caused by light, there certainly could not have been any people there without my seeing them." I agree that the "cluster" looks less like any natural flow of light, than a projection of the two figures forward—one seems to see the different levels of the heads. Though the mystery must remain unsolved, Mr. Hardy's photograph is one of great interest and beauty.

In the first sentence of my first chapter I regretted that I had never seen a ghost, adding that I might have heard one. It is time to explain that now. On October 27th, 1955, I received a letter from Calverton Rectory, Wolverton, Bucks, the relevant part of which read as follows: "I am proposing to go with a professional photographer to take night photographs at the old haunted Manor House at Abthorpe, of which we told you and sent you some snaps. We are making this expedition on Monday, 31st of October (Hallow'een). Would you be able to manage to join us? If so, will you make for this address on Monday next. The Rector says he will be very pleased if you will stay at the Rectory for the night." The two gentlemen concerned make a charming pair, an old man and a young man, the Rev. R. Bathurst Ravenscroft and Mr. L. E. Stotesbury-Leeson, whose bond, besides friendship, is the Ministry and their common devoted interest in Genealogical researches. Unfortunately, I was lecturing in Bournemouth on the evening of October 31st. I let them know my disappointment. The date was considerately changed for me, and I motored to Calverton Rectory on All Saints' Day, November 1st.

Mr. Stotesbury-Leeson is a direct descendant of the Leeson

family of Abthorpe, springing from those of Whitfield and Sulgrave which appear in the Heraldic Visitations of Northants as far back as the time of Edward I. Not until after the Reformation was the house—called Abthorpe Vicarage for very nearly the past two hundred years, but still to this day known to many as "Leeson Manor"—purchased by the Leeson family from the Ouseleys of Courteenhall near Northampton. It has remained part of the Jane Leeson trust from 1648, when "Mistress Jane Leeson died April ye 1st" as the simple record of the parish register runs. Little is known of "Mistress Jane," beyond the facts that she built the village school, which bears under one of its gables the inscriptions FEARE GOD AND HONOUR Y KING and JANE LEESON HATH BUILDED THIS HOUS FOR A FREE SCHOOL FOR EVER. 1642; made an endowment to the church to help provide a clergyman; left a charitable trust consisting of various annual bequests to a number of neighbouring parishes, and died a spinster. The payments began in 1649 and have continued regularly, the trustees meeting, until recent times, in the council chamber, as desired by Jane Leeson in her will.

This pre-Elizabethan Manor, empty and derelict, had fallen into a sad state of disrepair. On pushing open the warped gates, one stepped into a wilderness of undergrowth, the drive overshadowed by yews. Neglected lawns ran up to the worn stone walls; and, as one entered through the low Tudor doorway, one saw the long hallway, with dust-strewn rooms to left and right. The right-hand wing consisted of the Monastic Grange, the oldest part of the house. Here, in the council chamber Mr. Stotesbury-Leeson discovered in 1954 through the crumbling of the inner wall from damp, a curious chamber or cavity reaching down to the ground-floor, which looked like a "priest hole." From an attic a collapsed wall gave another view of the "priest hole" and the false wattled wall of the council chamber. Certainly the space within the wall could have concealed a man and might have been used, in times of religious persecution, as a refuge. The council chamber has its own eerie atmosphere. In this room there has been seen by one of the trustees and by others, the apparition of a Franciscan Friar. He is generally seated, reading a book; but on being disturbed, he glides across the chamber and disappears into the wall near the "priest hole."

Mr. Stotesbury-Leeson told me that very few of the villagers cared to pass by the house after sunset. On Sunday, October 31st, 1954, Mr. Bathurst Ravenscroft and he had taken some photographs of the outside of Leeson Manor in the middle of the afternoon. They made a tour of the house, ascending a narrow oak staircase to obtain a view of the "priest hole" concealed within the thickness of the walls. Mr. Stotesbury-Leeson writes:

"While I was investigating the inside of the 'priest hole' my companion, who was standing behind me, experienced the chill of some unseen presence, which passed off in a few moments but gave him the feeling that 'it' was there.

"We descended the stairs to the hall and went into the garden, intending later to return and make a further search of the house. Taking up positions on the lawn for photographing the exterior, I clearly sensed that something flashed past me, which quite startled me; and turning my head, I exclaimed 'What was that!' After about a minute (the front door being open) a door within the house, previously closed, opened and closed again with great violence. We sensed a feeling of psychic strain, so much so that we refrained from returning to the house. The sale of the property is in question and we had been discussing this topic.

"As the first member of the Leeson family to enter the house for three hundred years, I was photographed by Mr. Ravenscroft in the Tudor doorway. On having the photographs developed, a figure is clearly to be seen standing on my left-hand side, partly in the shadow and partly with the sun shining through it upon the stone lintel." I have three of the photographs in front of me. The first was taken at approximately 3 p.m. and shows the doorway quite clear. The second, taken at 3.10, reveals a figure on the right of the print, half on the sun-lit stonework, half in shadow. In the third photograph, taken a few minutes later from further away, the figure has moved a little more to the left but is not very distinct."

When I reached Calverton Rectory on the night of November 1st, 1955, the first thing I learnt was that the professional photographer had been prevented from coming, or perhaps had thought better of the expedition! However, he had lent his up-to-date camera and photographic equipment to Mr. Stotesbury-Leeson, who used an Ilford H.P.S. film, with a flash gun fitted to the camera. After supper we drove some fifteen freezing miles in brilliant moonlight to Abthorpe. Altogether we spent three full hours, from 9.15 p.m. until almost 12.30 a.m., making our investigation in the derelict, abandoned, yet not wholly forsaken, Manor House.

I may as well say at once that the photographs were a failure and revealed nothing paranormal. But Mr. Stotesbury-Leeson makes this comment: "Curiously enough the long exposures are mysteriously blotted out, in spite of the special film, the clear moonlight night, and the great care we took to adjust the camera each time we used it. These are the ones on which we set our hopes, and even now I feel that had the stills taken of the Tudor doorway been successful, you would have had at least one good photograph of a spectre."

"Not wholly forsaken"—because we both heard quite unaccountable sounds. There had been a full moon the night before: from a bitter cold clear sky, that brilliant dead world of dry terrible mountain-peaks looked down on us. As to the possibility of movement and any consequent noise, the air was as still as it could be. I am certain that there was not a breath, not a twig; and, no, not a rat nor a mouse stirring.

Mr. Stotesbury-Leeson heard more than I did, but this was probably my lack or defect. I felt no psychic chill or sense of unease when I crossed the threshold and entered the first room on the left of the hall. Neither did I feel fear nor discomfort in any other part of the house, only a detached but intense curiosity about what might happen next. I was hoping for proof; to see something.

My companion walked to the door and stood outside. I shone my torch, though the moonlight coming through the broken windows made this almost unnecessary. Suddenly I heard a noise, like a thump or muffled bark; but Mr. Stotesbury-Leeson, who heard it also, has described it as a "sort of scraping rushing sound." For a long time we heard nothing more, except the loud clang of a row of rusty bells that my friend set jangling with his walking stick!

Now we went upstairs into the Leeson council chamber where all seemed peaceful as we took several photographs, the camera pointing towards the "priest hole." We invoked Mistress Jane to reveal herself, with no result whatever. We then made separate circuits of the house, shining our torches everywhere, finding nothing unusual. But afterwards, on account of the noises each of our movements produced, we decided to keep together.

It was in a small room in the north-west corner of the first floor that we both heard the oddest sounds of all. I stood by the dusty mantelpiece, Mr. Stotesbury-Leeson closer to a half-open window of diamonded glass. It was bitterly cold and we drew our scarves and greatcoats tighter round us. Moonlight broke upon the diamond panes, faintly adulterating the room's darkness, light and shadow shafting down on walls and floor. We stood, for perhaps fifteen minutes, calm, transfixed, neither of us speaking or wanting to speak. The moments seemed long and it is difficult to be positively certain of what one heard. My ears, of course, may have built up imaginary noises, but I don't think they did. Whenever we had stopped talking, the silences could almost be heard. Then a sibilant sound came to me, like a small lisp, a lament, the whimper of water. A strange feeling tingled through the nerves of my skin.

Mr. Stotesbury-Leeson heard this, too, and something more; but he shall speak for himself: "I became aware of a noise like a dull groan with a roar, similar to a strong wind blowing through a small hole, which seemed to come from under my feet. The room below was the one where I had heard the first scraping rushing sound. I went downstairs, but now had the impression of hearing the same sound above me. I returned to the small north-west room upstairs and resumed my old position. After I had requested whatever spirits there might be to make themselves known, I noticed a faint sound as of running water which gradually increased in volume and seemed to come closer. It was only afterwards that I remembered that Mistress Jane Leeson had stated that she hoped her Charity would last 'For as long as the sun shines *and the water flows*,' a play on the family coat of arms." Mr. Stotesbury-Leeson thinks that his after-thought and theory about the water hits the nail on the head. Could that faint approaching Presence, if she was trying to make herself known to us by the sound of flowing water, have been his ancestor, Jane Leeson? As in so many occult matters we should be content to say we do not know. We must begin and end with a question mark, while we go on seeking.

But now it is time to set a term to our small inquiry about ghosts, which could be extended indefinitely. Maybe the strictly scientific lines upon which the S.P.R. today is working, with its praiseworthy aim of making psychical research respectable by drawing it into the laboratory, will prove most fruitful for man's advance into the Unknown. We live in a universe far more wonderful than any of us can fully contemplate, and the next stage of man's evolutionary development might well be—like wing from chrysalis—that of his psychical unfolding. Wise scientists have always recognised the limitations of science: in a subject so linked with spiritual, not to mention diabolical, knowledge we need not neglect other direct approaches, such as the mystical and the religious. If we are studying the whole of Reality, surely there need be no antithesis between spiritual and material existences, for they may interpenetrate. The scientific approach to these profound mysteries, though most valuable, is not the only one.